FARM JOURNAL'S
COUNTRY-STYLE
MICROWAVE
COOKBOOK

2

By the Food Editors of Farm Journal

FARM JOURNAL'S
COUNTRY-STYLE
MICROWAVE
COOKBOOK
2

By the Food Editors of Farm Journal

Farm Journal, Inc., Philadelphia, Pennsylvania

Book design: Ken Bittman
Cover photos: William Hazzard

Library of Congress Cataloging in Publication Data
Main entry under title:
Farm journal's country-style microwave cookbook 2.
Includes index.
1. Microwave cookery.
I. Farm journal (Philadelphia, Pa. :1956)
II. Title: Country-style microwave cookbook.
TX832.F377   1982   641.5'882   82-12025
ISBN 0-89795-014-3

CONTENTS

INTRODUCTION

Remember the first time you saw a microwave oven being used—or how intrigued you were the first time you saw someone microwave a potato in only 5 minutes, or warm a baby's bottle in just seconds?

Maybe it was your neighbor who introduced you to this new form of cookery when she told you she couldn't be without her microwave oven, especially on those days that just bustle with activity and family dinners often are eaten in shifts.

Clearly you'd found what every busy cook is seeking—the wherewithal to quick and convenient meal preparation. Soon you had a shiny new microwave oven of your very own, and with the use-and-care manual in hand, discovered the adventures of microwave cooking. As your confidence grew, so grew your repertoire of microwave recipes for chicken, ground beef, vegetables, and yes—even eggs.

Because the response to our first Country-style Microwave Cookbook was so strong, we decided to produce this second cookbook, with over 100 more country-style recipes to help you think of your microwave as an everyday appliance to use at every meal. We've included breakfast, lunch and dinner dishes, as well as vegetables, side dishes, breads and desserts—all full-flavored traditional favorites with microwave speed.

Each recipe in this book has been tested—around the kitchen table in farm homes across the country, and in the Farm Journal Test Kitchens, where our home economists double-checked every ingredient and every step. So even if you've never used a microwave oven before, we know these recipes will work for you, just as they did for us.

Ronnie J. Fulvi
Assistant Food Editor

CHAPTER ONE
GETTING THE MOST FROM YOUR MICROWAVE

Before you try our recipes for Curried Eggs with Bacon, Polynesian Pork, Pumpkin Cheese Pie, or any of the other great-tasting recipes in this collection, read through the pages that follow. Here we examine the principles of microwave cooking. We start with a brief description of how microwaves work and build on these basics with guidelines for selecting microwave accessories, plus lots of tips to help you get the most out of your microwave.

MICROWAVE COOKERY

You've probably heard it said that microwave cookery differs from conventional cooking because microwaved foods cook "from the inside out." But that's not exactly true. Foods prepared on top of the range or in the oven cook from the direct application of heat or heated air, which warms the surface of the food, then travels to the center.

Microwave cooking is unique because of the microwaves themselves—high-frequency electromagnetic waves which are absorbed by food directly to a depth of ¾ to 1½ inches. Here they cause the molecules of water, fat and sugar in the food to rub rapidly against each other and produce the heat that thaws, warms, or cooks the food—depending upon the length of cooking time you choose. Even after the oven is turned off and the microwaves are stopped, it takes a little more time for the action of the molecules to slow to a stop—so the food continues to cook. For this reason, many recipes suggest "let stand" for a few minutes before serving.

USING THESE RECIPES

Since the size of your oven's cavity and characteristics of the food all affect cooking time, you may need to adjust cooking times in these recipes. Each recipe in this book was tested in a 600- or 675-watt microwave oven. The output wattage of a microwave oven is a measure of its cooking power. If your microwave oven has an output of less than 600 watts, we suggest cooking the food the length of time specified in the recipe. If the food is not done, cook a little longer and check again. Most recipes in this book tell you when and how to check for doneness. If you're not sure of the wattage output of your microwave oven, check your use-and-care manual or ask your dealer.

Once a recipe specifies a temperature setting, such as high, continue to use that setting unless directed otherwise, even if you interrupt the cooking process to stir, add ingredients or rotate the dish. This same rule of thumb applies to coverings. Once directed to cover a utensil, continue to use the cover unless the recipe directs you to remove cover.

TIPS AND TECHNIQUES

Even if you're new to microwave cooking, most of the techniques you'll use will be familiar to you—they're the same ones used in conventional cooking. Although their application may differ, most help to speed cooking and promote even heating. Here are the most common ones.

Arrange food or utensils in a ring pattern to expose all sides to microwave energy for even cooking. If two items are cooked together, place one alongside the other. Arrange three items in a triangular pattern; place four items in a square.

Arrange *unevenly shaped foods* so that thinner, more delicate areas are toward the center and thicker parts are on the outside.

The thicker parts will receive more microwave energy and the food will be evenly cooked.

Covering foods helps to retain moisture, tenderize, speed cooking, and prevent spattering. Each recipe in this book indicates the type of cover to be used if one is needed. If the recipe says "cover and microwave," use the lid that comes with the casserole. If you don't have a lid, you can substitute plastic wrap.

When using plastic wrap, we suggest *venting*—turning back one corner of the wrap or cutting small slits to allow excess steam to escape—unless the recipe recommends otherwise. For best results, use the cover recommended in each recipe, and see "The Great Microwave Cover-up," p. 4.

Rearranging foods is done more often when microwaving because the corners or sides of utensils receive more energy than the center, and rearranging foods part way through the cooking period ensures even cooking. To rearrange foods in a utensil, simply bring foods from the outside of the utensil to the center, and vice versa. To rearrange individual utensils such as custard cups, just move them around and place in a new order. When foods need to be rearranged, we indicate this in the recipe.

Rotating, or turning a dish in the microwave, is used for foods which cannot otherwise be stirred, turned, or rearranged to help them to cook more evenly. Recipes tell exactly how to rotate—giving dish a one-quarter or one-half turn.

Shielding is used to protect sensitive areas (like poultry wing tips and breastbones) or to slow down cooking in spots which tend to cook more quickly than others, such as the corners of a square baking dish. Many manufacturers recommend shielding with small, smooth pieces of aluminum foil placed close to the food. However, check the use-and-care manual for your oven before using foil, because the magnetron tubes on some ovens can be damaged by foil.

Stirring cooked portions of food from the outside to the center of the dish helps equalize the food temperature and shorten cooking time.

Standing time is needed to complete the cooking process in many foods. If a food needs to be allowed to stand before serving, this is indicated in the recipe.

Turning large, dense foods—roasts or whole vegetables such as a head of cauliflower—helps ensure even cooking.

IT'S A MATTER OF TIMING

Speed is the most obvious advantage of microwave cooking, but in microwave cooking the difference between a juicy, tender piece of meat and one that is as tough as shoe leather can be a matter of seconds, so it's important to check food often.

Always use the *minimum* time when a range is given in a recipe. If only one time is given, check the food one minute before the total time specified. To help you decide whether the food is fully cooked, we've included a doneness test for most recipes. Remember that microwaved foods sometimes look underdone, but standing time completes the cooking process. Because the cooking time is so short, there's less margin of error in microwave cooking, so it's important to be aware of these factors.

Volume: The more food you're cooking, the longer it will take— in microwave cooking, time is directly related to quantity. When doubling a recipe, increase the time by half and check for doneness a minute before the total cooking time is completed.

Size: Small portions cook faster than large ones. Since microwaves penetrate foods ¾ to 1½ inches, uniform pieces less than two inches in diameter cook from all sides.

Shape: Thin parts of unevenly shaped foods cook faster than thick portions. Foods of uniform thickness cook evenly. Round shapes and rings cook more evenly.

Density: Dense foods such as potatoes take longer to microwave than light, porous foods such as cakes and breads.

Composition: Microwaves are attracted to foods high in moisture, fat and sugar, so those foods will cook more rapidly.

Starting temperature: Food that's at room temperature will cook faster than refrigerated or frozen foods. Cooking times in our recipes are based on the temperature at which the food is normally stored.

Bone: Bone conducts heat, causing meat closest to the bone to cook more rapidly than other parts. Boneless cuts cook less rapidly, but more evenly.

THE GREAT MICROWAVE COVER-UP

When it comes to microwave cooking, knowing how and when to use covers can be the difference between success and failure. Generally, foods that require covers in conventional cooking should be covered during microwaving. Several materials can be used—each serving specific functions. Deciding *which* foods to cover *when* and with *what* should be determined by the food itself and the desired result of the final food product.

Glass covers trap steam and moisture, retain heat, and are used like plastic wrap. Glass lids are most suitable for vegetables, casseroles and meats which need steam for tenderizing.

Paper towels and napkins prevent spattering, absorb moisture and fat and promote even cooking. When cooking bacon, notice how the paper towels act as a blotter. Paper toweling is an effective cover for saucy vegetable casseroles, sandwiches and fish or poultry with a bread crumb coating.

Plastic wrap helps retain heat and moisture, speed cooking and promote even cooking. Use plastic wrap when microwaving vegetables, casseroles, fish and meats which require steam for tenderizing. Select a wrap that can withstand high temperatures and one that clings well to utensils made from a variety of materials. Be careful in removing plastic wrap from dishes, because a build-up of steam could burn you. To be safe, cut tiny slits in the wrap or vent the wrap by turning back one of the corners.

Waxed paper helps retain heat and allows steam to escape. Use it with foods that don't need to be tenderized—chicken, ground meat patties, soups and fruits.

REHEATING

If you're an experienced microwave cook, you know that foods reheated in the microwave have that fresh-cooked taste, not a warmed-over one. In fact, some dishes, like soups and stews, taste even better when the flavors are allowed to mellow and blend in the refrigerator overnight.

To prevent overcooking when reheating foods, use a medium-high power setting, or about 70% power. And remember, foods at room temperature reheat faster than refrigerated dishes.

To test for doneness, feel the bottom of the plate. When it feels warm, the foods are hot enough to transfer warmth to the plate and are ready to serve. Another guide is to allow 1½ to 2 minutes cooking time for each cup of mixture, or when moisture is visible inside the cover. Allow reheated foods a standing time of at least one minute before eating, to assure even temperature.

CHOOSING MICROWAVE UTENSILS

We've tested all the recipes in this book in standard glass oven-safe dishes that are also microwave-safe, so you don't need to stock up on special microwave cooking utensils. In fact, many utensils you already have may be well suited for microwaving—oven-safe glass casseroles, pie plates and baking dishes, glass measuring cups, mixing bowls and custard cups. And it's so convenient to measure, mix, cook and even serve in one bowl.

Before using any utensil in your microwave oven, give it the look-and-see test. Turn the utensil over and look for a label reading "Suitable for Microwave" or "Microwave Oven Safe." If the utensil is not labeled and you want to be sure it's microwave-safe, try this simple test: Fill a glass measuring cup with 8 oz. of water and place it inside the empty dish you are testing. Microwave at high setting 1 to 2 minutes. If the dish is still cool but the water is hot, the dish is suitable for microwaving.

The best utensils for microwave cooking, heating and defrosting are those which allow the microwave energy to pass through the material to the food. Heat-resistant glass, glass ceramic (without metal trim or screws in the lids or handles), some plastics, and paper products work well. Stoneware, porcelain and china without decorative metallic trim also are suitable.

As the popularity of microwave ovens continues to increase, more and more accessories have appeared, and new ones are being introduced all the time. With so many to choose from, it's hard to know which will provide the most satisfaction. To help you decide, ask yourself the following questions before you buy:

• How versatile is the accessory and how often will I be able to use it? Can it go from microwave to conventional cooking?

• How tolerant is it to temperature changes? Will it go from oven to freezer to microwave oven to dishwasher? Accessories must be temperature-resistant up to 300 degrees.

• What about the size and shape of the container? The depth is as important as the capacity because a shallow container exposes more food surface to the microwave energy, therefore cooking it faster. Round shapes cook more evenly than square or rectangular. Casseroles with straight sides will keep depth of food uniform.

• Does it have handles? Remember that some things do get hot in your microwave oven.

• How heavy is the accessory—both empty and filled?

CHAPTER TWO
BREAKFAST, BRUNCH OR LUNCH

BACON-WRAPPED SHIRRED EGGS

12 strips bacon
6 eggs

⅓ c. shredded Cheddar
cheese

Place a layer of paper towels in 12x8x2" (2-qt.) glass baking dish. Arrange bacon in 3 layers in baking dish, separating each layer with a paper towel. (End with a paper towel.)

Microwave (high setting) 3 minutes. Rotate dish one-quarter turn. Microwave 3 minutes more. Set aside.

Butter 6 (6-oz.) glass custard cups. Circle inside edge of each cup with 2 strips bacon. Break an egg into the center of each and prick egg yolks with a wooden pick. Sprinkle eggs with cheese.

Arrange custard cups in ring in microwave oven. Cover with waxed paper.

Microwave (medium setting) 2 minutes. Rearrange custard cups. Microwave 2 minutes more, or until egg whites are set but egg yolks are still soft. Makes 6 servings.

CURRIED EGGS WITH BACON

1 (13¾-oz.) can chicken
  broth
Milk
12 strips bacon
3 tblsp. butter or regular
  margarine
¼ c. finely chopped onion
¼ c. finely chopped celery
¼ c. finely chopped green
  pepper

5 tblsp. flour
1 tsp. curry powder
¹/₈ tsp. pepper
6 hard-cooked eggs,
  sliced
9 slices buttered toast,
  cut in half diagonally

Pour chicken broth into measuring cup. Add enough milk to make 3 c.; set aside. Arrange half the bacon in 12x8x2" (2-qt.) glass baking dish, overlapping to fit. Cover with waxed paper.

Microwave (high setting) 3 minutes. Rotate baking dish one-quarter turn and separate bacon strips with a fork. Microwave 2 to 3 minutes more, or until bacon is nearly done. Remove and drain on paper towels. Pour off and reserve bacon drippings. Repeat with remaining bacon.

Place 3 tblsp. reserved bacon drippings and butter in 2-qt. glass casserole. Microwave (high setting) 1 minute, or until butter melts. Add onion, celery and green pepper. Cover and microwave (high setting) 5 minutes or until tender.

Blend in flour, curry powder and pepper. Microwave (high setting), uncovered, ½ minute. Gradually stir in chicken broth mixture. Microwave (high setting) 3 minutes. Stir. Microwave 5 minutes more, or until sauce thickens, stirring after each minute.

Stir in sliced eggs. Microwave 1 minute more or until hot. For each serving, arrange 3 toast halves on a plate. Top with 2 strips bacon and ⅔ c. curried egg mixture. Makes 6 servings.

CREOLE OMELET

½ c. chopped onion	½ c. water
½ c. chopped green pepper	1 drop Tabasco sauce
1 clove garlic, minced	¼ tsp. salt
2 tblsp. cooking oil	⅛ tsp. pepper
1 (8-oz.) can stewed tomatoes	3 tblsp. butter or regular margarine
1 (8-oz.) can tomato sauce	8 eggs
1 (4-oz.) can sliced mushrooms	3 tblsp. milk
	¼ tsp. salt
	⅛ tsp. pepper
	Grated Parmesan cheese

Combine onion, green pepper, garlic and oil in 12x8x2" (2-qt.) glass baking dish. Cover with waxed paper. Microwave (high setting) 4 minutes. Stir. Microwave 4 minutes more or until tender.

Stir in tomatoes, tomato sauce, undrained mushrooms, water, Tabasco sauce, ¼ tsp. salt and ⅛ tsp. pepper. Cover with waxed paper. Microwave (high setting) 4 minutes. Stir. Microwave 4 minutes more. Set aside.

Place 1½ tblsp. of the butter in 9" glass pie plate. Microwave 1 minute or until melted. Beat together eggs, milk, ¼ tsp. salt and ⅛ tsp. pepper in bowl until well blended, using a fork.

Pour half of the egg mixture into pie plate. Microwave (medium setting) 3 to 4 minutes. Lift edge with spatula and tilt pie plate so uncooked portion flows underneath. Microwave 2 to 4 minutes more or until almost set. Loosen omelet with turner and fold in half. Invert onto warm platter. Pour half of the sauce over omelet; sprinkle with cheese. Repeat with remaining butter, egg mixture, sauce and cheese. Makes 4 servings.

FRENCH HAM SANDWICHES

4 eggs	**½ lb. thinly sliced cooked**
1 c. milk	**ham**
½ tsp. vanilla	**Sugar**
8 slices white bread	**Ground cinnamon**
4 tsp. shortening	**Maple syrup**

Combine eggs, milk and vanilla in bowl. Beat until smooth, using a rotary beater. Dip bread into egg-milk mixture, coating both sides well, using all of the egg-milk mixture.

Preheat microwave browning dish according to manufacturer's directions. Place 1 tsp. shortening on hot browning dish and let melt. Add 2 slices of bread.

Microwave (high setting) 30 seconds. Turn bread and microwave 30 seconds more or until browned. Repeat with remaining shortening and bread, preheating browning dish each time by microwaving (high setting) 2 minutes or until hot.

Place 4 slices of French toast in 12x8x2" (2-qt.) glass baking dish. Place one-fourth of the ham on each slice of French toast. Top with remaining toast. Cover with waxed paper.

Microwave (high setting) 3 minutes or until hot, rotating dish one-quarter turn after each minute. Sprinkle with sugar and cinnamon. Serve with maple syrup. Makes 4 servings.

CORN BREAD 'N' SAUSAGE

12 pork sausage links (about 12 oz.)	2 eggs
1 c. sifted flour	¼ c. honey
1 c. yellow corn meal	¼ c. cooking oil
¼ c. wheat germ	1 (8-oz.) container plain yogurt
4 tsp. baking powder	Honey Butter (recipe follows)
½ tsp. salt	

Preheat microwave browning dish according to manufacturer's directions. Place sausages in browning dish and microwave (high setting) 3 minutes. Turn sausages and microwave 3 minutes more or until browned. Remove from dish and drain on paper towels.

Stir together flour, corn meal, wheat germ, baking powder and salt. Set aside.

Combine eggs, honey, oil and yogurt in a small bowl; blend well. Add all at once to dry ingredients, stirring just enough to moisten. Pour batter into greased 12x8x2″ (2-qt.) glass baking dish. Arrange sausages on top of batter. Place in microwave oven on an inverted saucer.

Microwave (medium setting) 3 minutes. Rotate dish one-quarter turn. Microwave 3 minutes more. Rotate dish one-quarter turn.

Microwave (high setting) 2 to 4 minutes, or until a wooden pick inserted in center comes out clean, rotating dish one-quarter turn after 2 minutes. Let stand directly on counter 5 minutes.

Meanwhile, prepare Honey Butter. Cut corn bread into squares and serve with warm Honey Butter. Makes 6 servings.

Honey Butter: Combine ½ c. butter or regular margarine and ⅔ c. honey in glass bowl. Microwave (high setting) 3 minutes, or until mixture comes to a boil. Microwave 30 seconds more.

FRUIT AND NUT BREAKFAST BARS

3 c. quick-cooking oats
2 c. flaked coconut
1 c. sliced almonds
½ c. coarsely chopped
   walnuts
1 c. golden raisins
½ c. coarsely chopped,
   pitted dates

½ c. chopped dried
   apricots
½ c. unsifted flour
½ tsp. salt
3 eggs, slightly beaten
¾ c. honey
⅓ c. cooking oil

Sprinkle half of the oats, coconut, almonds and walnuts in a 12x8x2" (2-qt.) glass baking dish. Microwave (high setting) 8 minutes or until toasted, stirring every 3 minutes. Repeat with remaining oats, coconut, almonds and walnuts. Cool well.

Combine oat mixture, raisins, dates, apricots, flour and salt in bowl. Stir in eggs, honey and oil, mixing well. Press into 2 greased 8" square glass baking dishes. Place pieces of foil over the corners of each dish.

Place one dish in microwave oven on an inverted saucer. Microwave (high setting) 6 minutes, rotating dish one-quarter turn every 2 minutes. Cool directly on counter. Repeat with remaining dish. Cut into 2" squares. Makes 32 bars or 16 servings.

ZUCCHINI-SHRIMP SCRAMBLE

1 (4½-oz.) can small
  shrimp, drained
3 tblsp. butter or regular
  margarine
2 c. finely chopped
  zucchini

⅓ c. chopped onion
6 eggs
¼ tsp. salt
¼ tsp. pepper

Rinse shrimp with cold water. Soak shrimp in bowl of iced water 20 minutes. Drain well; set aside.

Place 1 tblsp. of the butter in 1½-qt. glass casserole. Microwave (high setting) 30 seconds. Add zucchini and onion. Cover and microwave 2 minutes. Stir. Microwave 2 minutes more.

Add shrimp. Cover and microwave (high setting) 1 minute. Place mixture in large sieve and drain.

Beat eggs, salt and pepper in bowl until well blended.

Place remaining 2 tblsp. butter in same 1½-qt. casserole. Microwave (high setting) 30 seconds. Add egg mixture. Microwave 1½ minutes, stirring every 30 seconds. Stir in zucchini-shrimp mixture. Microwave 45 seconds, stirring once. Let stand 2 minutes. Makes 4 servings.

ZUCCHINI-CHEDDAR QUICHE

Golden Pie Shell (recipe
  follows)
2 eggs
1¼ c. evaporated milk
¼ tsp. salt
1 c. shredded Cheddar
  cheese

⅔ c. thinly sliced
  zucchini
2 tblsp. thinly sliced
  green onions
Ground nutmeg

Prepare Golden Pie Shell. Beat eggs in bowl, using a rotary beater. Add evaporated milk and salt; blend well. Stir in cheese, zucchini and green onions. Pour into greased 8" glass pie plate.

Microwave (medium setting) 8 minutes, stirring every 3 minutes. Sprinkle with nutmeg. Microwave 8 to 12 minutes more, or until a knife inserted halfway between the center and edge comes out clean, rotating plate one-quarter turn every 2 minutes. Cool on counter until set, about 15 minutes.

Carefully pull custard away from plate, using a small spatula. Gently shake pie plate to loosen custard. Tilt plate over Golden Pie Shell, with far edge of filling just above far edge of pie shell. Slip the custard into pie shell, pulling the plate back toward you until all the filling settles into place. Makes 4 to 6 servings.

Golden Pie Shell: Combine 1 c. sifted flour and ½ tsp. salt in bowl. Cut in 6 tblsp. margarine until coarse crumbs form. Add 2 to 3 tblsp. iced water, tossing with a fork until dough forms; press firmly into a ball. Roll out dough on floured surface to 12" circle. Fit into 8" pie plate. Trim to 1" beyond rim of pie plate. Fold under edge and flute. Prick surface of pie shell with a fork.

Microwave (high setting) 2 minutes. Rotate plate one-quarter turn. Microwave 2 to 4 minutes, or until crust is dry and opaque. (Cover any brown spots with small pieces of foil.) Cool on rack.

CHICKEN DIVAN ON TOAST

2 whole chicken breasts, split	1/8 tsp. pepper
1/4 c. flour	1/2 c. shredded Swiss cheese
2 c. milk	1/3 c. grated Parmesan cheese
2 chicken bouillon cubes	
1/2 tsp. Worcestershire sauce	1 1/2 lb. fresh broccoli
1/4 tsp. dry mustard	1/2 c. water
1/8 tsp. ground nutmeg	6 slices buttered toast
	Paprika

Arrange chicken in 8″ square glass baking dish, skin side down, with meatiest parts to outside of dish. Cover with waxed paper. Microwave (high setting) 5 minutes. Turn chicken over and rearrange. Cover and microwave 4 minutes more, or until tender. Remove chicken; reserve drippings.

Combine flour and milk in jar. Cover and shake until blended. Stir flour mixture into drippings. Add bouillon cubes, Worcestershire sauce, mustard, nutmeg and pepper. Microwave (high setting) 8 minutes, or until sauce thickens, stirring after each minute. Add Swiss and Parmesan cheese, stirring until melted. Set aside.

Cut broccoli into spears with 1″ flowerets and 3″ stems. Arrange broccoli in 12x8x2″ (2-qt.) glass baking dish with flowerets to center of dish. Add water. Cover with plastic wrap, turning back one corner. Microwave (high setting) 2 minutes. Rotate dish one-quarter turn. Microwave 2 minutes more. Remove broccoli and rinse dish. Remove chicken from bones and slice.

Place toast in same 2-qt. baking dish. Top with chicken, broccoli and cheese sauce. Sprinkle with paprika. Microwave (high setting) 4 minutes. Rotate dish one-quarter turn. Microwave 4 minutes more. Makes 6 servings.

CHICKEN CREOLE

¾ c. chopped onion
¾ c. chopped celery
¾ c. chopped green
  pepper
1 clove garlic, minced
¼ c. butter or regular
  margarine
2½ c. cut-up, cooked
  chicken
1 (16-oz.) can stewed
  tomatoes

1 (6-oz.) can tomato paste
2 tblsp. chopped fresh
  parsley
2 tsp. Worcestershire
  sauce
½ tsp. salt
⅛ tsp. pepper
1 bay leaf
4 drops Tabasco sauce
1½ c. water
Hot cooked rice

Combine onion, celery, green pepper, garlic and butter in 3-qt. glass casserole. Cover and microwave (high setting) 8 minutes.

Stir in remaining ingredients except rice. Cover and microwave (high setting) 8 minutes. Remove cover and microwave 2 minutes more. Remove bay leaf. Serve over hot cooked rice. Makes 6 servings.

CREAMED HAM WITH PEAS

½ c. finely chopped onion
⅓ c. butter or regular
    margarine
6 tblsp. flour
½ tsp. dry mustard
⅛ tsp. pepper
3⅓ c. milk
1 (8-oz.) pkg. cream
    cheese, cubed
3 c. cooked ham strips

1 (10-oz.) pkg. frozen
    peas, cooked and
    drained (2 c.)
1 (4-oz.) can sliced
    mushrooms, drained
½ tsp. Worcestershire
    sauce
Hot biscuits

Combine onion and butter in 3-qt. glass casserole. Microwave (high setting) 4 minutes or until tender. Blend in flour, mustard and pepper. Gradually stir in milk. Microwave (high setting) 5½ to 6 minutes, or until sauce boils and thickens, stirring every 2 minutes.

Add cream cheese, stirring until melted. Stir in ham, peas, mushrooms and Worcestershire sauce. Microwave (high setting) 2 minutes. Stir. Microwave 2 minutes more or until hot. Serve over hot biscuits. Makes 6 servings.

GERMAN-STYLE POTATO SALAD WITH FRANKS

½ lb. bacon, diced
¾ c. chopped onion
3 tblsp. sugar
3 tblsp. flour
1 tsp. celery seed
¾ c. cider vinegar
1½ c. water

6 c. sliced, cooked
potatoes (about 3 lb.)
8 frankfurters, sliced
2 hard-cooked eggs,
sliced
Chopped fresh parsley

Place bacon in 12x8x2″ (2-qt.) glass baking dish. Cover with plastic wrap, turning back one corner to let steam escape. Microwave (high setting) 3 minutes. Stir. Microwave 2 minutes more or until crisp. Remove bacon and drain on paper towels. Pour off all but ⅓ c. bacon drippings.

Add onion to drippings. Cover with plastic wrap, turning back one corner. Microwave (high setting) 2 minutes. Stir. Microwave 2 minutes more or until tender.

Stir in sugar, flour and celery seed. Slowly stir in vinegar and water. Microwave (high setting), uncovered, 4 minutes, or until mixture thickens, stirring after each minute.

Stir in potatoes, frankfurters and bacon. Microwave (high setting) 4 minutes or until hot. Garnish with sliced eggs and parsley. Makes 8 servings.

SEAFOOD POTATO TOPPER

⅓ c. butter or regular
margarine
2 tblsp. flour
¼ tsp. paprika
2 c. milk
1 c. shredded Cheddar
cheese
½ tsp. Worcestershire
sauce

4 egg yolks, beaten
1 lb. white fish fillets,
cooked and cut up
1 (4½-oz.) can shrimp,
drained
4 baked potatoes

Place butter in 3-qt. glass casserole. Microwave (high setting) 1 minute or until melted. Blend in flour and paprika. Gradually stir in milk. Microwave (high setting) 5 minutes, or until sauce thickens, stirring every 2 minutes. Add cheese and Worcestershire sauce, stirring until cheese melts.

Stir some of the hot sauce into egg yolks. Stir egg yolk mixture back into hot sauce. Microwave (medium setting) 4 minutes, or until sauce thickens, stirring after each minute.

Stir in fish and shrimp. Microwave (medium setting) 2 to 3 minutes or until hot, stirring after each minute. Serve over baked potatoes. Makes 4 servings.

TUNA TOMATO SAUCE FOR PASTA

1 (28-oz.) can Italian
    tomatoes
¼ c. chopped green
    pepper
¼ c. chopped onion
3 cloves garlic, minced
2 tblsp. cooking oil
1 (8-oz.) can tomato
    sauce
1 (6-oz.) can tomato paste
⅓ c. water
½ tsp. salt

½ tsp. dried oregano
    leaves
½ tsp. dried basil leaves
¼ tsp. ground nutmeg
¼ tsp. sugar
⅛ tsp. pepper
1 (7-oz.) can solid-pack
    tuna, drained and
    flaked
1 lb. pasta, cooked and
    drained

Purée tomatoes in blender until smooth; set aside.

Combine green pepper, onion, garlic and oil in 2-qt. glass casserole. Cover and microwave (high setting) 2 minutes. Stir. Microwave 1 minute more.

Stir in puréed tomatoes, tomato sauce, tomato paste, water, salt, oregano, basil, nutmeg, sugar and pepper. Cover and microwave (high setting) 10 minutes. Stir. Microwave 10 minutes more.

Stir in tuna. Cover and microwave (high setting) 2 minutes. Serve over cooked pasta. Makes 8 servings.

DOUBLE-CHEESE MACARONI

1 c. uncooked elbow
  macaroni
3 c. very hot water
1 tsp. salt
¼ c. butter or regular
  margarine
1½ c. milk
1 c. soft bread crumbs
1 c. shredded Cheddar
  cheese
½ c. shredded Swiss
  cheese

½ c. thinly sliced cooked
  ham
3 eggs, slightly beaten
1 tblsp. finely chopped
  onion
1 tblsp. chopped fresh
  parsley
¼ tsp. salt
⅛ tsp. pepper
Paprika

Combine macaroni, hot water and 1 tsp. salt in 2-qt. glass casserole. Cover and microwave (high setting) 10 minutes. Stir. Microwave 5 minutes more, or until macaroni is tender. Drain in colander.

Return hot macaroni to casserole. Add butter and toss until macaroni is coated.

Pour milk into 4-c. glass measuring cup. Microwave (high setting) 4 minutes or until scalded.

Add scalded milk, bread crumbs, Cheddar cheese, Swiss cheese, ham, eggs, onion, parsley, ¼ tsp. salt and pepper to macaroni mixture; mix well. Cover.

Microwave (high setting) 3 minutes, or until outside edge is set and center is slightly soft, stirring after each minute. Sprinkle with paprika. Let stand 5 minutes before serving. Makes 4 servings.

BACON-CHEESE MACARONI

6 strips bacon, cut into
  ½ " pieces
½ c. chopped onion
1 (10¾-oz.) can con-
  densed cream of mush-
  room soup
1 c. milk
7 to 8 oz. elbow or
  corkscrew macaroni,
  cooked and drained

1½ c. shredded Long-
  horn-style mild Ched-
  dar or Colby cheese
1½ c. shredded Cheddar
  cheese
1 (10-oz.) pkg. frozen
  peas, thawed (2 c.)
2 tblsp. diced pimiento
1 tblsp. chopped fresh
  parsley

Place bacon and onion in 2-qt. glass casserole. Cover and microwave (high setting) 4 minutes. Stir. Microwave 4 minutes more, or until bacon is crisp. Add soup and milk, blending well.

Add remaining ingredients and toss gently to mix well. Cover.

Microwave (high setting) 15 minutes or until hot and bubbly, stirring every 5 minutes. Makes 6 servings.

EGGPLANT IN A POCKET

1½ c. sliced onion
1 clove garlic, minced
½ tsp. paprika
½ tsp. ground cumin
2 tblsp. butter or regular
  margarine
1 (1-lb.) eggplant, cut into
  ¾ " cubes
¼ lb. fresh mushrooms,
  sliced

½ c. chopped green
  pepper
1 (16-oz.) can stewed
  tomatoes, drained
1 (10¾-oz.) can con-
  densed golden
  mushroom soup
4 drops Tabasco sauce
12 pita bread, cut in half
Shredded Cheddar cheese

Combine onion, garlic, paprika, cumin and butter in 3-qt. glass casserole. Cover and microwave (high setting) 5 minutes.

Stir in eggplant, mushrooms and green pepper. Cover and microwave (high setting) 5 minutes. Stir. Microwave 5 minutes more, or until eggplant is tender.

Stir in drained tomatoes, mushroom soup and Tabasco sauce. Cover and microwave (high setting) 3 minutes or until hot. Spoon into pita bread. Sprinkle filling with cheese. Makes 12 sandwiches or 6 servings.

BROCCOLI AND NOODLES

1½ lb. fresh broccoli
½ c. water
½ tsp. salt
½ c. chopped onion
1 clove garlic, minced
2 tblsp. butter or regular
   margarine
3 tblsp. flour
1¼ c. milk
2 tblsp. chopped fresh
   parsley

½ tsp. salt
½ tsp. dried oregano
   leaves
1½ c. creamed small-curd
   cottage cheese
1 c. shredded Cheddar
   cheese
¼ c. grated Romano
   cheese
8 oz. noodles, cooked and
   drained

Remove flowerets from broccoli and cut larger ones in half lengthwise. Cut stems into 1″ lengths.

Combine broccoli, water and ½ tsp. salt in 3-qt. glass casserole. Cover and microwave (high setting) 9 minutes or until tender, stirring every 3 minutes. Let stand, covered, 2 minutes. Drain in colander.

Place onion, garlic and butter in same casserole. Cover and microwave (high setting) 3 minutes. Blend in flour. Gradually stir in milk. Add parsley, ½ tsp. salt and oregano. Microwave (high setting) 1 minute. Stir. Microwave 1 minute more.

Stir in cottage cheese. Microwave (high setting) 2 minutes. Stir. Microwave 2 minutes more, or until cottage cheese is almost melted. Add Cheddar and Romano cheese; stir well. Microwave 1 minute or until melted.

Add broccoli. Cover and microwave (high setting) 1 minute or until hot. Serve over noodles. Makes 6 servings.

FETTUCINI ALFREDO

8 oz. uncooked fettucini or medium noodles	1²/₃ c. light cream
2 qt. very hot water	¾ c. grated Parmesan cheese
1 tblsp. salt	2 tblsp. chopped fresh parsley
6 tblsp. butter or regular margarine	⅛ tsp. pepper
1 clove garlic, minced	Chopped fresh parsley

Combine fettucini, hot water and salt in 3-qt. glass casserole. Cover and microwave (high setting) 10 minutes. Stir. Cover and microwave 12 minutes more or until tender. Drain noodles in colander and keep warm.

Place butter in 2-qt. glass casserole. Microwave (high setting) 1 minute or until melted. Add garlic and microwave 1 minute more. Stir in cream. Microwave 4 minutes or until hot.

Stir in Parmesan cheese, 2 tblsp. parsley and pepper. Arrange noodles on serving platter. Pour sauce over noodles, tossing to coat. Garnish with chopped parsley. Makes 6 servings.

CHEESY HAMBURGER PIZZA

Pizza Crusts
(recipe follows)
Hamburger Pizza Sauce
(recipe follows)
1 c. shredded mozzarella
cheese

⅓ c. grated Romano or
Parmesan cheese
½ c. sliced pimiento-
stuffed olives

Prepare Pizza Crusts and Hamburger Pizza Sauce. Spread crusts with sauce. Top with cheeses and olives. Microwave (high setting) 1 pizza at a time 5 minutes. Makes 2 (9″) pizzas.

Pizza Crusts: Dissolve 1 tsp. active dry yeast in 3 tblsp. lukewarm water (110°) in bowl. Stir in ¼ c. warm milk, 1 tblsp. sugar, 2 tblsp. butter, ½ tsp. salt, 3 drops yellow food coloring and ½ c. sifted flour. Stir in ½ to ¾ c. sifted flour, or enough to make a soft dough. Turn out onto floured surface and knead until smooth. Place in greased bowl, turning over once to grease top. Cover and let rise in warm place until doubled, about 45 minutes.

Punch down dough and divide in half. Roll out each half to 10″ circle. Brush 2 (9″) glass pie plates with 1 tblsp. melted butter and sprinkle with 2 tblsp. crumbs. Fit dough into prepared pie plates. Brush with 1 tblsp. melted butter and sprinkle with ¾ c. dry bread crumbs. Cover and let rise until doubled, 20 minutes.

Prick one crust several times with fork. Microwave (medium setting) 4 to 6 minutes, or until crust is dry, rotating plate one-half turn every 2 minutes. Repeat with remaining crust.

Hamburger Pizza Sauce: Crumble ½ lb. ground chuck into 1½-qt. glass casserole. Add ½ c. chopped onion and 1 clove garlic (minced). Cover and microwave (high setting) 3 minutes, stirring once. Stir in 1 (8-oz.) can tomato sauce, 1 (6-oz.) can tomato paste and ½ tsp. Italian seasoning. Microwave 3 minutes.

SOUTHWESTERN CHILI BUNS

1½ lb. ground chuck
¾ c. chopped onion
½ c. chopped green
  pepper
1 clove garlic, minced
2 (8-oz.) cans tomato
  sauce
½ c. ketchup

¼ c. chopped fresh
  parsley
2 tblsp. chili powder
½ tsp. salt
⅛ tsp. Tabasco sauce
4 hamburger buns, split
Shredded Cheddar cheese

Combine ground chuck, onion, green pepper and garlic in 3-qt. glass casserole. Microwave (high setting) 8 minutes, or until meat loses its pink color, stirring every 3 minutes. Pour off fat.

Stir in tomato sauce, ketchup, parsley, chili powder, salt and Tabasco sauce. Microwave (high setting) 4 minutes. Stir. Microwave 3 minutes more or until hot and bubbly. Serve on hamburger buns and sprinkle with cheese. Makes 4 servings.

MOZZARELLA MEATBALL SANDWICHES

1 lb. ground chuck	¾ c. ketchup
¼ c. chopped onion	1 (4-oz.) can mushroom
1 egg	stems and pieces
½ tsp. salt	½ tsp. Italian herb
¼ tsp. pepper	seasoning
16 (½″) cubes mozzarella	1 clove garlic, minced
cheese	4 (10″) Italian rolls, split

Combine ground chuck, onion, egg, salt and pepper in bowl. Mix lightly, but well. Divide mixture into 16 portions. Press each portion around a cheese cube and shape into a meatball. Place meatballs in 12x8x2″ (2-qt.) glass baking dish.

Microwave (high setting) 3 minutes. Turn meatballs and rearrange by moving outside meatballs to center. Microwave 3 to 4 minutes more or until set. Pour off fat. Cover with waxed paper and let stand while preparing sauce.

Combine ketchup, undrained mushrooms, Italian seasoning and garlic in 2-qt. glass casserole. Cover.

Microwave (high setting) 3 minutes. Stir. Microwave 2 minutes more or until hot and bubbly. Pour sauce over meatballs, stirring gently. Spoon 4 meatballs with sauce into each Italian roll. Makes 4 servings.

TACO SALAD

1 c. dairy sour cream
1 c. mayonnaise
1 (1-oz.) env. buttermilk
  ranch dressing mix
1 lb. ground chuck
1 (1¼-oz.) env. taco
  seasoning mix
¾ c. water
1 head iceberg lettuce,
  torn into bite-size
  pieces (10 c.)

2 medium tomatoes, cut
  into 8 wedges each
1 c. sliced celery
½ c. sliced ripe olives
1½ c. shredded Cheddar
  cheese
½ (9-oz.) pkg. taco-
  flavored tortilla chips,
  coarsely crushed

Combine sour cream, mayonnaise and buttermilk ranch dressing mix in bowl; mix well. Cover and refrigerate at least 30 minutes.

Crumble ground chuck into 1-qt. glass casserole. Cover and microwave (high setting) 2 minutes. Stir. Microwave 2 minutes more, or until meat loses its pink color. Pour off fat.

Stir in taco seasoning mix and water. Microwave (high setting), uncovered, 5 minutes. Stir. Microwave 5 minutes more.

Combine hot meat mixture with remaining ingredients in salad bowl. Toss to mix. Serve immediately with chilled dressing. Makes 6 servings.

CHAPTER THREE

DINNER WITH A DIFFERENCE

OLD WORLD SAUERBRATEN

1 (3 to 3½-lb.) boneless
  beef rump roast
1 c. cider vinegar
1 c. water
¼ c. packed brown sugar
2 tsp. salt
¼ tsp. pepper
¼ tsp. ground cloves

1 c. chopped onion
1 c. shredded, pared
  carrots
1 c. chopped celery
1 bay leaf
¼ c. gingersnap crumbs
¼ tsp. browning for gravy
½ c. dairy sour cream

Place roast in 3-qt. glass casserole. Combine vinegar, water, brown sugar, salt, pepper and cloves in another bowl; mix well. Pour mixture over beef. Turn beef to coat all sides. Add onion, carrots, celery and bay leaf. Cover and marinate in refrigerator for 2 days, turning roast several times.

Remove casserole from refrigerator and place in microwave oven. Microwave (medium setting) 30 minutes. Turn roast over. Microwave 30 to 45 minutes more or until tender.

Remove roast and keep warm. Skim fat from surface of broth. Strain broth and discard bay leaf. Place cooked vegetables and ½ c. of the broth in blender. Cover and blend until smooth.

Combine vegetable mixture, remaining broth, gingersnap crumbs and browning for gravy in same casserole.

Microwave (high setting) 2 minutes, or until gravy is slightly thickened.

Stir some of the hot gravy mixture into sour cream. Then stir sour cream mixture back into casserole. Slice roast and serve with gravy. Makes 6 to 8 servings.

BEEF AND GREEN BEAN STIR-FRY

1 lb. boneless beef sirloin
  steak
½ tsp. salt
⅛ tsp. pepper
½ lb. fresh green beans,
  cut into 1″ diagonal
  lengths
1 c. chopped onion
2 cloves garlic, minced
½ c. water

2 beef bouillon cubes
1 tsp. dried basil leaves
½ tsp. salt
1 tblsp. cornstarch
2 tblsp. water
2 medium tomatoes,
  peeled and cut into
  8 wedges each
½ tsp. browning for gravy

Freeze beef slightly. Thinly slice partially frozen beef into 2½x¼″ strips. Season with ½ tsp. salt and pepper; set aside.

Combine green beans, onion, garlic, ½ c. water, bouillon cubes, basil and ½ tsp. salt in 2-qt. glass casserole. Cover and microwave (high setting) 4 minutes. Stir. Microwave 4 minutes more.

Add beef. Cover and microwave (high setting) 3 minutes. Stir. Microwave 3 to 5 minutes more, or until beef loses its pink color. Drain beef mixture, reserving juices in 2-c. glass measuring cup.

Combine cornstarch and 2 tblsp. water in small bowl; stir until blended. Add to reserved juices. Microwave (high setting) 3 minutes, or until sauce thickens.

Stir sauce, tomatoes and browning for gravy into beef mixture. Microwave 1 minute more or until hot. Makes 4 servings.

ROUND STEAK
WITH MUSHROOM GRAVY

2 lb. beef round steak,
  ½ " thick
⅓ c. flour
2 tsp. paprika
1 tsp. salt
¼ lb. fresh mushrooms,
  sliced
⅔ c. sliced onion

1 small clove garlic,
  minced
2 tblsp. cooking oil
1 c. water
⅔ c. dairy sour cream
1 tblsp. chopped fresh
  parsley

Pound beef to about ¼" thickness and cut into 6 pieces. Combine flour, paprika and salt. Dredge beef in flour mixture, reserving any leftover flour mixture.

Combine mushrooms, onion, garlic and oil in 12x8x2" (2-qt.) glass baking dish. Cover with plastic wrap, turning back one corner to let steam escape.

Microwave (high setting) 3 minutes. Stir. Microwave 3 minutes more, or until vegetables are tender. Add beef to baking dish, spooning vegetables over beef. Sprinkle with reserved flour mixture. Pour water over all. Cover tightly with plastic wrap. (Do not vent.)

Microwave (medium setting) 25 minutes. Turn beef over and rearrange by moving outside pieces to center of dish. Cover tightly and microwave 25 minutes more, or until beef is tender.

Remove beef to serving platter and keep warm. Skim fat from surface of juices. Stir some of the hot juices into sour cream. Then stir sour cream mixture back into remaining juices.

Microwave (medium setting) 1 minute. Spoon some of the gravy over beef and sprinkle with parsley. Pass remaining gravy. Makes 6 servings.

TEXICAN CHILI

3 strips bacon, diced
½ c. finely chopped onion
¼ c. finely chopped green
  pepper
¼ c. finely chopped celery
1 clove garlic, minced
1 lb. boneless beef round,
  cut into ½" cubes
1 (15-oz.) can red kidney
  beans
1 (16-oz.) can tomatoes,
  cut up

1 (8-oz.) can tomato
  sauce
¼ c. thinly sliced, pared
  carrots
1 tblsp. finely chopped
  fresh parsley
½ bay leaf
1 tblsp. chili powder
½ tsp. salt
¼ tsp. ground cumin
Dash of pepper

Combine bacon, onion, green pepper, celery and garlic in 3-qt. glass casserole. Cover and microwave (high setting) 3 minutes. Stir. Microwave 3 minutes more, or until bacon is crisp and vegetables are tender.

Stir in remaining ingredients. Cover and microwave (medium setting) 35 minutes. Stir. Microwave 40 minutes more, or until beef is tender. Remove bay leaf. Makes 4 servings.

BEEF PAPRIKA

1½ lb. boneless beef
  round, about ¾ " thick
1 tsp. salt
¼ tsp. pepper
½ lb. fresh mushrooms,
  sliced
1½ c. chopped onion
1 clove garlic, minced
4 tblsp. butter or regular
  margarine

4½ tsp. paprika
1 beef bouillon cube
½ c. water
1 c. light cream
2 tblsp. flour
1 c. dairy sour cream
Hot buttered noodles

Freeze beef slightly. Thinly slice partially frozen beef and season with salt and pepper. Set aside.

Place mushrooms, onion, garlic and butter in 2-qt. glass casserole. Cover and microwave (high setting) 4 minutes or until tender.

Add beef, paprika, bouillon cube and water. Cover and microwave (high setting) 5 minutes.

Reduce power to medium. Microwave (medium setting) 25 minutes. Stir. Microwave 25 minutes more, or until beef is tender.

Combine light cream and flour in jar. Cover and shake until blended. Stir into beef mixture. Microwave (medium setting) 5 minutes, or until sauce thickens, stirring every 2 minutes.

Stir some of the hot mixture into sour cream. Then stir sour cream mixture back into remaining hot mixture. Microwave (medium setting) 2 minutes or until hot. Serve over noodles. Makes 6 servings.

BEEF-NOODLE CASSEROLE

1 lb. ground chuck
¼ c. finely chopped onion
1 clove garlic, minced
2 (8-oz.) cans tomato
  sauce
1 tsp. salt
¼ tsp. pepper
1 c. dairy sour cream
1 c. creamed small-curd
  cottage cheese

1 c. sliced, cooked
  carrots
¼ c. chopped fresh
  parsley
8 oz. medium noodles,
  cooked and drained
1 c. shredded Cheddar
  cheese

Crumble ground chuck into 3-qt. glass casserole. Add onion and garlic. Cover and microwave (high setting) 3 minutes. Stir. Microwave 3 minutes more, or until beef loses its pink color. Pour off fat.

Stir in tomato sauce, salt and pepper. Microwave (high setting) 2 minutes, or until mixture begins to bubble.

Stir sour cream, cottage cheese, carrots and parsley into meat mixture. Add noodles and toss to coat.

Microwave (high setting) 5 minutes. Rotate casserole one-half turn. Microwave 5 to 7 minutes more or until hot. Sprinkle with Cheddar cheese. Microwave 2 minutes, or until cheese melts. Makes 6 servings.

BEEF 'N' EGG LOAVES

1½ lb. ground chuck	¼ tsp. paprika
¼ c. wheat germ	⅛ tsp. pepper
¼ c. finely chopped onion	1 egg, slightly beaten
¼ c. chopped fresh parsley	¼ c. milk
	¼ c. ketchup
1 tsp. salt	6 hard-cooked eggs
¼ tsp. dried thyme leaves	Sweet-Sour Sauce
¼ tsp. dry mustard	(recipe follows)

Combine all ingredients except hard-cooked eggs and Sweet-Sour Sauce in bowl. Mix lightly, but well. Divide mixture into 6 portions. Press each portion around a hard-cooked egg, forming a loaf. Place loaves in 12x8x2" (2-qt.) glass baking dish. Microwave (high setting) 7 minutes.

Meanwhile, prepare Sweet-Sour Sauce. Rearrange loaves and spoon Sweet-Sour Sauce over loaves.

Microwave (high setting) 7 minutes more, or until meat loses its pink color. Makes 6 servings.

Sweet-Sour Sauce: Combine ¼ c. ketchup, 1 tblsp. vinegar, 1 tblsp. packed brown sugar and ½ tsp. dry mustard in bowl; mix well.

STUFFED WHOLE CABBAGE

1 (2-lb.) head green
  cabbage
1 lb. lean ground chuck
1 (8-oz.) can tomato
  sauce
⅓ c. quick-cooking rice

1 egg, slightly beaten
1 env. onion soup mix
¾ tsp. dried thyme leaves
Velvety Cheese Sauce
  (recipe follows)

Remove core from cabbage and hollow out to form a 1″-thick shell.

Combine remaining ingredients, except Velvety Cheese Sauce, in bowl. Mix lightly, but well. Spoon into cabbage shell. Place in 1½-qt. glass casserole. Cover tightly with plastic wrap. (Do not vent.)

Microwave (high setting) 9 minutes. Rotate dish one-quarter turn. Microwave 8 to 10 minutes more. Let stand 10 minutes.

Meanwhile, prepare Velvety Cheese Sauce. Cut cabbage into 6 wedges and pour Velvety Cheese Sauce over cabbage. Makes 6 servings.

Velvety Cheese Sauce: Place 3 tblsp. butter or regular margarine in glass bowl. Microwave (high setting) 1 minute or until melted. Blend in 3 tblsp. flour, ¼ tsp. salt and ⅛ tsp. pepper. Gradually stir in 1½ c. milk. Microwave 5 minutes, or until sauce thickens, stirring after each minute. Add 1 c. shredded Cheddar cheese and stir until melted.

STUFFED CABBAGE ROLLS

1 (3-lb.) head green cabbage	1 clove garlic, minced
½ c. water	¼ tsp. dried thyme leaves
¾ lb. ground chuck	1 tsp. salt
1 c. cooked rice	⅛ tsp. pepper
¾ c. finely chopped onion	1 (28-oz.) can tomatoes,
¾ c. shredded, pared carrots	cut up
	1 (15-oz.) can tomato sauce
¾ c. milk	1 tsp. dried thyme leaves
1 egg, slightly beaten	3 tblsp. flour
⅓ c. finely chopped fresh parsley	⅓ c. water

Remove core from cabbage and place cabbage in 3-qt. glass casserole. Add ½ c. water. Cover with plastic wrap, turning back one corner to let steam escape. Microwave (high setting) 12 minutes, or until leaves are soft. Drain and cool slightly.

Pull 12 leaves away gently, one at a time. Drain on paper towels. Trim off thick part of leaves for easier rolling.

Combine next 11 ingredients in bowl; mix lightly, but well. Place ¼ c. meat filling on each cabbage leaf. Fold sides over filling and roll up, securing with a wooden pick. Place in same 3-qt. casserole. Stir in tomatoes, tomato sauce and 1 tsp. thyme. Cover. Microwave (high setting) 30 minutes, or until tender, stirring every 10 minutes. Remove cabbage rolls to serving bowl; keep warm.

Combine flour and water in jar. Cover and shake until blended. Stir flour mixture into sauce in casserole. Microwave (high setting) 9 minutes, or until sauce thickens, stirring every 3 minutes. Pour sauce over cabbage rolls. Makes 6 servings.

MEATBALL AND BEAN STEW

1 lb. ground chuck	2 (15-oz.) cans red kidney
½ c. soft bread crumbs	beans
¼ c. finely chopped onion	1 (28-oz.) can Italian
3 tblsp. finely chopped	tomatoes, cut up
fresh parsley	1 (15-oz.) can tomato
1 tsp. salt	sauce
½ tsp. dried oregano	1 bay leaf
leaves	½ tsp. dried oregano
¼ tsp. dried basil leaves	leaves
1 egg, slightly beaten	½ tsp. dried basil leaves
¼ c. milk	3 tblsp. cornstarch
1 c. green pepper strips	⅓ c. water
2 tsp. cooking oil	Shredded Cheddar cheese

Combine ground chuck, bread crumbs, onion, parsley, salt, ½ tsp. oregano, ¼ tsp. basil, egg and milk in bowl. Mix lightly, but well. Shape mixture into 32 meatballs. Arrange meatballs in 12x8x2″ (2-qt.) glass baking dish and set aside.

Combine green pepper and oil in 3-qt. glass casserole. Cover and microwave (high setting) 3 minutes. Stir in undrained kidney beans, tomatoes, tomato sauce, bay leaf, ½ tsp. oregano and ½ tsp. basil. Cover and microwave 16 minutes, stirring every 5 minutes. Set aside.

Microwave (high setting) meatballs 5 minutes. Turn meatballs over and rearrange. Microwave 5 minutes more or until firm. Remove meatballs with slotted spoon; stir into tomato mixture.

Combine cornstarch and water in small bowl; stir until blended. Add to meatball mixture. Cover and microwave (high setting) 2 minutes. Stir. Microwave 2 minutes more, or until sauce thickens. Serve topped with shredded cheese. Makes 10 servings.

HEARTY BEEF AND BEAN STEW

1½

2 lb. ground chuck
½ c. chopped onion
1 clove garlic, minced
1 tblsp. dried parsley
flakes
2 tsp. salt
1 tsp. dried basil leaves
½ tsp. pepper
1 (28-oz.) can tomatoes,
cut up *16 oz*

6 medium potatoes,
pared and cut into
¾" cubes (4 c.)
1 (16-oz.) can pork and
beans in tomato sauce
2 c. peas, fresh or frozen
and thawed

Crumble ground chuck into 3-qt. glass casserole. Cover and microwave (high setting) 3 minutes. Stir in onion, garlic, parsley flakes, salt, basil and pepper. Microwave (high setting) 5 minutes more, or until meat loses its pink color. Pour off fat. Stir in tomatoes. Do not cover.

Microwave (high setting) 15 minutes, stirring every 5 minutes. Stir in potatoes and pork and beans. Cover.

Microwave (high setting) 20 minutes, or until potatoes are tender, stirring every 7 minutes. Add peas. Cover and microwave 5 minutes more, or until peas are tender. Makes 8 servings.

POLENTA WITH MEAT SAUCE

1 tblsp. butter or regular margarine	½ lb. ground chuck
3 tblsp. chopped onion	¼ c. chopped onion
1 c. yellow corn meal	2 tblsp. chopped green pepper
1 tsp. salt	1 clove garlic, minced
1 tsp. sugar	¾ tsp. dried basil leaves
3¾ c. very hot water	¼ tsp. salt
1 (15-oz.) can red kidney beans, drained	⅛ tsp. pepper
1½ c. shredded Cheddar cheese	1 (16-oz.) can tomatoes
	1 (8-oz.) can tomato sauce

Place butter in 2-qt. glass casserole. Microwave (high setting) 1 minute. Add 3 tblsp. chopped onion. Cover and microwave 2 minutes or until tender. Remove onion.

Combine corn meal, 1 tsp. salt and sugar in same 2-qt. casserole. Stir in hot water. Microwave (high setting) 4 minutes. Stir. Microwave 3 minutes, or until mixture thickens. Add cooked onion, kidney beans and ½ c. of the cheese; stir until cheese melts. Pour into 8" square baking pan. Cover and refrigerate 1 hour. Crumble ground chuck into same 2-qt. casserole. Add next 7 ingredients. Cover and microwave (high setting) 3 minutes.

Purée tomatoes in blender. Stir tomatoes and tomato sauce into meat mixture. Cover and microwave (high setting) 6 minutes. Stir. Microwave, uncovered, 6 minutes more.

Cut corn meal mixture into 12 squares. Place in 12x8x2" (2-qt.) glass baking dish. Add meat mixture. Cover with waxed paper. Microwave (high setting) 16 minutes, rotating dish one-quarter turn every 4 minutes. Uncover. Sprinkle with remaining 1 c. cheese. Microwave 1 minute. Makes 6 servings.

UPSIDE-DOWN HAMBURGER SUPPER

Corn Bread Topping
  (recipe follows)
1 (10-oz.) pkg. frozen
  succotash
2 tblsp. water
¼ tsp. salt
¼ c. sliced ripe olives

1 lb. ground chuck
¾ c. chopped onion
1 clove garlic, minced
½ c. ketchup
½ tsp. dried thyme leaves
½ tsp. salt

Prepare Corn Bread Topping and set aside.

Combine succotash, water and ¼ tsp. salt in 3-qt. glass casserole. Cover and microwave (high setting) 2 minutes. Stir. Microwave 2 minutes more. Drain succotash and turn into bowl. Stir in olives and set aside.

Crumble ground chuck into same 3-qt. casserole. Add onion and garlic. Cover and microwave (high setting) 2 minutes. Stir. Microwave 2 minutes more. Pour off fat. Stir in ketchup, thyme and ½ tsp. salt. Push beef mixture to sides of casserole, forming a ring. Pour succotash mixture into center of ring.

Microwave (high setting) 2 minutes. Spread Corn Bread Topping evenly over all. Microwave (medium setting) 12 minutes, rotating dish one-quarter turn every 4 minutes.

Microwave (high setting) 4 minutes, or until top springs back when touched with finger. Let stand 5 minutes. Loosen edge and invert on serving platter. Makes 6 servings.

Corn Bread Topping: Combine 1 c. yellow corn meal, 1 c. sifted flour, 4 tsp. baking powder, ½ tsp. salt, ¼ c. packed brown sugar and ½ c. shredded Cheddar cheese in bowl. Add 1 c. milk, ¼ c. cooking oil and 1 beaten egg. Stir just until moistened.

SOUTHWESTERN-STYLE PORK CHOPS

4 pork chops, ½" thick　　**1 c. finely crushed taco-**
⅓ c. taco sauce　　　　　　　**flavored tortilla chips**

Dip both sides of pork chops in taco sauce and then in crushed tortilla chips, coating well. Place pork chops in 12x8x2" (2-qt.) glass baking dish, with meaty sides to outside of dish. Cover with waxed paper.

Microwave (medium setting) 8 minutes. Rotate dish one-quarter turn. Microwave 8 to 10 minutes more, or until pork is tender and meat near the bone is no longer pink. Makes 4 servings.

POLYNESIAN PORK

1 (8¼-oz.) can sliced
  pineapple
Water
½ c. packed brown sugar
3 tblsp. cornstarch
⅔ c. cider vinegar
4 tsp. soy sauce
1½ lb. boneless pork, cut
  into 2x⅛" strips
½ tsp. salt
⅛ tsp. pepper

1 clove garlic, minced
2 small onions, cut into
  8 wedges each
1 c. bias-cut celery
2 chicken bouillon cubes
1 medium green pepper,
  cut into strips
1 (11-oz.) can mandarin
  orange segments,
  drained

Drain pineapple, reserving juice. Add enough water to juice to make 1¼ c. Cut pineapple slices into quarters and set aside.

Combine brown sugar, cornstarch, vinegar and soy sauce in bowl. Stir to blend; set aside.

Season pork with salt and pepper. Place pork and garlic in 3-qt. glass casserole. Cover and microwave (medium setting) 10 to 12 minutes, or until pork loses its pink color, stirring every 3 minutes.

Stir in 1¼ c. pineapple juice, cornstarch mixture, onions, celery and bouillon cubes. Microwave (high setting) 5 minutes. Stir. Microwave 5 to 7 minutes more, or until sauce thickens and celery is tender-crisp, stirring every 2 minutes. Add green pepper and microwave 3 minutes or until tender-crisp.

Stir in orange segments and pineapple. Microwave (high setting) 1 minute more or until hot. Makes 6 servings.

HAM AND BROCCOLI ROYALE

1½ lb. fresh broccoli	3 c. milk
¼ c. water	4 c. cubed cooked ham
6 tblsp. butter or regular margarine	2 c. cooked rice
	1 (8-oz.) pkg. sliced
2 c. soft bread crumbs	pasteurized process
2 c. chopped onion	American cheese
3 tblsp. sifted flour	
¼ tsp. pepper	

Remove leaves from broccoli. Discard tough end of lower stalk. Wash broccoli and cut into flowerets with stalks 1″ thick.

Arrange broccoli in 12x8x2″ (2-qt.) glass baking dish with flowerets to center of dish. Sprinkle with ¼ c. water. Cover with plastic wrap, turning back one corner to let steam escape. Microwave (high setting) 6 minutes. Rotate dish one-half turn. Microwave 9 to 11 minutes more or until tender- crisp. Set aside.

Place butter in 3-qt. glass casserole. Microwave (high setting) 2 minutes or until melted. Place bread crumbs in bowl and drizzle 2 tblsp. of the melted butter over them. Toss to mix and set aside.

Add onion to remaining butter in casserole and microwave (high setting) 2 minutes. Stir. Microwave 2 minutes more, or until onion is tender. Blend in flour and pepper. Gradually stir in milk. Microwave (high setting) 3 minutes; stir. Microwave 6 minutes, or until sauce thickens, stirring after each minute. Stir in ham. Microwave (high setting) 2 minutes. Pour ham mixture into a bowl.

To assemble dish, spoon rice into 3-qt. glass casserole. Layer broccoli on top. Pour ham mixture over all. Top with cheese; sprinkle with bread crumbs. Microwave (high setting) 8 minutes. Rotate dish one-half turn. Microwave 7 minutes or until hot. Makes 8 servings.

CREAMY HAM AND POTATO DINNER

5 c. sliced, pared
   potatoes (¼" thick)
1 lb. fresh green beans,
   cut into 1" lengths
1 c. chopped celery
½ tsp. salt
¾ c. water
Milk
¼ c. butter or regular
   margarine

1 c. chopped onion
¼ c. flour
2 c. cubed, cooked ham
2 tblsp. chopped fresh
   parsley
1½ c. shredded Cheddar
   cheese

Combine potatoes, green beans and celery in 3-qt. glass casserole. Dissolve salt in water. Pour over vegetables. Cover and microwave (high setting) 8 minutes. Stir. Microwave 7 minutes more, or until vegetables are tender. Drain vegetables and set aside, reserving cooking liquid.

Add enough milk to cooking liquid to make 2½ c. Set aside.

Place butter in same 3-qt. casserole. Microwave (high setting) 30 seconds or until melted. Add onion and flour; blend well. Microwave 1 minute. Stir. Microwave 1 minute more. Gradually stir in milk mixture. Microwave (high setting) 5 minutes. Stir. Microwave 5 minutes more, or until sauce thickens, stirring after each minute.

Stir in drained vegetables, ham and parsley. Cover.

Microwave (high setting) 15 minutes or until hot, rotating dish one-quarter turn every 5 minutes. Sprinkle with cheese. Microwave 1 minute more, or until cheese melts. Makes 6 servings.

✓ CHILI AND CORN BREAD SUPPER

2 (15½-oz.) cans chili
   with beans
2 c. cubed, cooked ham
1 (28-oz.) can tomatoes,
   cut up
1 (16-oz.) can mixed
   vegetables, drained
2 tblsp. instant minced
   onion

¾ tsp. chili powder
1 (12-oz.) pkg. corn
   muffin mix
2 tblsp. grated Parmesan
   cheese
1 egg, beaten
½ c. milk

Combine chili, ham, tomatoes, mixed vegetables, onion and chili powder in 3-qt. glass casserole; mix well. Cover.

Microwave (high setting) 15 minutes or until hot, stirring every 5 minutes.

Meanwhile, combine remaining ingredients in bowl. Stir just enough to moisten.

Drop batter by spoonfuls onto hot stew. Microwave (high setting) 6 minutes. Rotate dish one-half turn. Microwave 3 minutes more, or until a wooden pick inserted in corn bread topping comes out clean. Makes 6 to 8 servings.

EXTRA-EASY LASAGNE

1 (28-oz.) can Italian
tomatoes, cut up
1 (6-oz.) can tomato paste
2 tblsp. chopped fresh
parsley
1 tsp. dried oregano
leaves
½ tsp. dried basil leaves
1 lb. bulk pork sausage
½ c. chopped onion

1 clove garlic, minced
1 (1½-oz.) pkg. spaghetti
sauce mix
1 (16-oz.) container
creamed large-curd
cottage cheese
4 c. uncooked medium
noodles
8 oz. shredded mozzarella
cheese

Purée tomatoes with tomato paste in blender until smooth. Stir in parsley, oregano and basil; set aside.

Break up sausage with wooden spoon in 12x8x2″ (2-qt.) glass baking dish. Stir in onion and garlic. Cover with waxed paper.

Microwave (high setting) 4 minutes. Stir. Microwave 4 minutes more, or until sausage loses its pink color. Pour off fat. Stir in half of the spaghetti sauce mix.

Spoon cottage cheese evenly over sausage mixture. Arrange noodles on top. Sprinkle with remaining spaghetti sauce mix. Pour tomato mixture over noodles. Press down gently with spoon to be sure all the noodles are moistened. Cover with waxed paper.

Microwave (high setting) 10 minutes. Rotate dish one-quarter turn. Microwave 10 minutes more, or until noodles are tender. Sprinkle with mozzarella cheese. Microwave, uncovered, 2 minutes more, or until cheese melts. Makes 8 servings.

FRANK AND NOODLE DINNER

½ c. sliced green onions
 with tops
1 clove garlic, minced
2 tblsp. cooking oil
8 oz. uncooked wide
 noodles
2 c. very hot water
1 tsp. salt
1 c. creamed cottage
 cheese

1 c. dairy sour cream
1 (8-oz.) can tomato
 sauce
1 lb. frankfurters
1 c. shredded Cheddar
 cheese
¼ c. chopped fresh
 parsley

Combine green onions, garlic and oil in 12x8x2″ (2-qt.) glass baking dish. Cover with waxed paper. Microwave (high setting) 2 minutes. Add noodles, water and salt. Cover with waxed paper. Microwave (high setting) 5 minutes. Stir. Microwave 5 minutes more, or until noodles are tender. Drain any excess water from noodles.

Stir together cottage cheese, sour cream and tomato sauce in bowl. Stir into noodles.

Slit frankfurters lengthwise, cutting almost through. Stuff with Cheddar cheese. Arrange stuffed frankfurters on top of noodles. Cover with waxed paper.

Microwave (high setting) 9 minutes, rotating dish one-half turn every 3 minutes. Sprinkle with parsley. Makes 6 servings.

INDOOR-BARBECUED CHICKEN

½ c. chopped onion
½ c. chopped celery
1 tblsp. cooking oil
1 (10¾-oz.) can
    condensed tomato soup
1 c. ketchup
¼ c. lemon juice
3 tblsp. Worcestershire
    sauce

3 tblsp. packed brown
    sugar
2 tblsp. vinegar
2 tblsp. prepared mustard
¼ tsp. pepper
2 drops Tabasco sauce
1 (3-lb.) broiler-fryer,
    quartered

Combine onion, celery and oil in 1½-qt. glass casserole. Cover and microwave (high setting) 3 minutes. Stir in remaining ingredients except for chicken. Cover and microwave (high setting) 3 minutes. Stir. Microwave 3 minutes more.

Dip chicken quarters in barbecue sauce, coating well on all sides. Reserve remaining barbecue sauce. Arrange dipped chicken in 12x8x2" (2-qt.) glass baking dish, skin side down, with meatiest parts to outside of dish. Cover with waxed paper.

Microwave (high setting) 10 minutes. Turn chicken over and move outside pieces to center of dish. Baste with barbecue sauce, reserving remaining sauce. Cover with waxed paper. Microwave 9 minutes more, or until chicken is tender and meat near the bone is no longer pink. Let stand 5 minutes. Meanwhile, microwave remaining barbecue sauce (high setting) 3 minutes or until hot. Pass sauce with chicken. Makes 4 servings.

CHICKEN IN HONEY SAUCE

3 whole chicken breasts,
   split (about 3 lb.)
1 tsp. salt
¼ tsp. pepper
1 (20-oz.) can pineapple
   chunks in juice
2 c. bias-cut, pared
   carrots
⅓ c. chopped onion
⅓ c. water

½ c. cider vinegar
⅓ c. honey
1 tblsp. soy sauce
2 chicken bouillon cubes
¼ c. cornstarch
½ c. water
1 (6-oz.) pkg. frozen pea
   pods, thawed
Hot cooked rice

Season chicken breasts with salt and pepper. Place chicken in 12x8x2" (2-qt.) glass baking dish, skin side down, with meatiest parts to outside of dish. Cover with plastic wrap, turning back one corner to let steam escape.

Microwave (high setting) 8 minutes. Turn chicken over and move outside pieces to center of dish.

Drain pineapple, reserving juice. Add pineapple juice, carrots, onion, ⅓ c. water, vinegar, honey, soy sauce and bouillon cubes to chicken. Cover with plastic wrap, turning back one corner. Microwave (high setting) 8 to 10 minutes, or until chicken is tender and meat near the bone is no longer pink. Remove chicken; keep warm.

Combine cornstarch and ½ c. water in bowl; stir to blend. Stir cornstarch mixture into baking dish. Microwave (high setting) 3 minutes, or until sauce thickens, stirring after every minute. Stir in pea pods and pineapple chunks. Microwave (high setting) 1 minute more or until hot.

Arrange chicken and vegetables on rice. Spoon some sauce over chicken; pass remaining sauce. Makes 6 servings.

CHICKEN BREASTS IN CREAM SAUCE

3 whole chicken breasts,
  split (about 3 lb.)
1/4 c. butter or regular
  margarine
1/2 c. chopped onion
2 tblsp. flour
1/2 tsp. dried basil leaves
1/4 tsp. paprika
1/4 tsp. salt

1/8 tsp. ground nutmeg
1/8 tsp. pepper
1 (8 3/4-oz.) can whole-
  kernel corn
1/3 c. milk
1 1/2 c. dairy sour cream
2 tblsp. chopped
  pimiento
Chopped fresh parsley

Arrange chicken in 12x8x2" (2-qt.) glass baking dish, skin side down, with meatiest parts to outside of dish. Dot with butter and sprinkle with onion. Cover with plastic wrap, turning back one corner to let steam escape.

Microwave (high setting) 8 minutes. Turn chicken over and move outside pieces to center of dish. Microwave 7 to 10 minutes more, or until chicken is tender and meat near the bone is no longer pink.

Remove chicken from dish. Skim fat from drippings. Add flour, basil, paprika, salt, nutmeg and pepper to drippings. Gradually stir in undrained corn and milk.

Microwave (high setting) 3 minutes. Stir. Microwave 3 minutes more, or until sauce thickens, stirring after each minute.

Stir some of the hot mixture into sour cream. Then stir sour cream mixture back into dish. Stir in pimiento.

Microwave (high setting) 2 minutes. (Do not boil.) Pour sauce over chicken and sprinkle with parsley. Makes 6 servings.

CURRIED CHICKEN WITH RICE

¼ lb. fresh mushrooms, sliced
¾ c. green pepper strips
½ c. chopped onion
1 clove garlic, minced
2 tblsp. cooking oil
Very hot water
1 (10½-oz.) can condensed chicken broth

1 c. uncooked regular rice
1 tsp. curry powder
1 chicken bouillon cube
2 small whole chicken breasts, split
½ tsp. salt
1 (6-oz.) pkg. frozen pea pods, thawed
1 medium tomato, chopped

Combine mushrooms, green pepper, onion, garlic and oil in 12x8x2" (2-qt.) glass baking dish. Cover with plastic wrap, turning back one corner to let steam escape. Microwave (high setting) 2 minutes.

Add enough hot water to chicken broth to make 2¼ c. Stir chicken broth, rice, curry powder and bouillon cube into vegetable mixture. Cover with plastic wrap, turning back one corner. Microwave (high setting) 4 minutes. Stir. Microwave 3 minutes more.

Season chicken breasts with salt. Arrange on top of rice mixture.

Cover with plastic wrap, turning back one corner to let steam escape. Microwave (high setting) 18 minutes, rotating dish one-quarter turn every 4 minutes. Remove chicken and keep warm.

Stir pea pods and tomato into rice mixture. Microwave (high setting) 1 minute. Arrange chicken on top of rice mixture and serve immediately. Makes 4 servings.

GOLDEN LASAGNE

2 tblsp. butter or regular margarine
¼ lb. fresh mushrooms, sliced
½ c. finely chopped onion
½ c. chopped green pepper
1 (10¾-oz.) can condensed cream of chicken soup
3 tblsp. milk
¼ c. chopped pimiento

½ tsp. dried basil leaves
8 lasagne noodles (8 oz.), cooked and drained
1 c. creamed small-curd cottage cheese
2 c. cubed, cooked chicken
1½ c. shredded Cheddar cheese
⅓ c. grated Parmesan cheese

Place butter in 1-qt. glass casserole. Microwave (high setting) 1 minute or until melted. Add mushrooms, onion and green pepper. Cover and microwave (high setting) 4 minutes or until tender. Stir in chicken soup, milk, pimiento and basil.

Arrange 4 noodles in greased 12x8x2" (2-qt.) glass baking dish. Top with half of the sauce, half of the cottage cheese, half of the chicken, half of the Cheddar cheese and half of the Parmesan cheese. Arrange remaining noodles on top and repeat layers. Cover with waxed paper.

Microwave (high setting) 18 minutes or until hot and bubbly, rotating dish one-quarter turn every 4½ minutes. Let stand 10 minutes before serving. Makes 6 servings.

CHICKEN 'N' RICE

1 c. chopped celery
½ c. chopped onion
½ c. butter or regular
   margarine
Very hot water
2 (10¾-oz.) cans
   condensed chicken
   broth
1 c. uncooked regular rice

1½ c. diced, pared carrots
½ tsp. salt
⅛ tsp. pepper
⅛ tsp. powdered saffron
3 c. cubed, cooked
   chicken
¼ c. chopped fresh
   parsley

Combine celery, onion and butter in 12x8x2" (2-qt.) glass baking dish. Cover with plastic wrap, turning back one corner to let steam escape.

Microwave (high setting) 2 minutes. Stir. Microwave 2 minutes more or until tender.

Add enough hot water to chicken broth to make 3½ c. Add chicken broth mixture, rice, carrots, salt, pepper and saffron to baking dish. Cover with plastic wrap, turning back one corner.

Microwave (high setting) 12 minutes. Stir. Microwave 13 minutes more, or until rice is tender. Stir in chicken and parsley. Microwave 2 minutes more or until hot. Makes 6 servings.

SWEET-AND-SOUR CHICKEN

1 (20-oz.) can pineapple
  chunks in juice
Water
½ c. packed brown sugar
¼ c. cornstarch
½ tsp. ground ginger
½ c. cider vinegar

¼ c. soy sauce
1¼ c. green pepper strips
1 c. sliced onion
1 c. sliced, pared carrots
2 c. cubed, cooked
  chicken
Hot cooked rice

Drain pineapple, reserving juice. Add enough water to juice to make 2½ c.

Combine brown sugar, cornstarch and ginger in 3-qt. glass casserole. Gradually stir in 2½ c. pineapple juice, vinegar and soy sauce.

Microwave (high setting) 10 minutes, or until sauce thickens, stirring every 2 minutes. Add pineapple, green pepper, onion, carrots and chicken. Cover and microwave 20 minutes, or until vegetables are tender-crisp, stirring every 5 minutes. Serve with rice. Makes 6 servings.

TURKEY TETRAZZINI

2 c. heavy cream
½ c. chopped onion
4 tblsp. butter or regular
  margarine
4 tblsp. flour
½ tsp. salt
¼ tsp. pepper
2 c. chicken broth
2 c. cubed, cooked turkey
1 c. grated Parmesan
  cheese

2 (4-oz.) cans mushroom
  stems and pieces,
  drained
⅓ c. chopped fresh
  parsley
½ c. toasted slivered
  almonds
8 oz. spaghetti, cooked
  and drained
Chopped fresh parsley

Place cream in 4-c. glass measuring cup. Microwave (high setting) 1½ minutes or until warm; set aside.

Place onion and butter in 12x8x2" (2-qt.) glass baking dish. Cover with waxed paper and microwave (high setting) 3 minutes. Stir. Microwave 3 minutes more or until tender.

Blend in flour, salt and pepper. Gradually stir in chicken broth. Microwave (high setting) 3 minutes. Stir. Microwave 5 minutes more, or until sauce thickens, stirring after each minute. Gradually stir in warm cream.

Stir in turkey, cheese, mushrooms, ⅓ c. parsley and ¼ c. of the almonds.

Toss spaghetti with turkey mixture in large bowl. Turn back into baking dish. Sprinkle with remaining almonds.

Microwave (high setting) 2½ minutes. Rotate dish one-quarter turn. Microwave 2½ minutes more or until hot and bubbly. Sprinkle with parsley. Makes 6 servings.

CURRIED TURKEY WITH RICE

1 c. sliced onion
1 apple, pared, cored and
   sliced
¼ c. bias-cut, pared
   carrots
¼ c. bias-cut celery
1 clove garlic, minced
¼ c. butter or regular
   margarine
⅓ c. flour
2 tblsp. curry powder
¼ tsp. ground ginger
¼ tsp. ground mace

⅛ tsp. pepper
2 c. chicken broth
1 (4-oz.) can sliced
   mushrooms
3 c. cubed, cooked turkey
2 c. dairy sour cream
Hot cooked rice
Condiments: Chopped
   onion, green pepper,
   tomato, hard-cooked
   eggs, roasted peanuts,
   raisins, coconut,
   chutney

Combine onion, apple, carrots, celery, garlic and butter in 12x8x2" (2-qt.) glass baking dish. Microwave (high setting) 3 minutes. Stir. Microwave 3 minutes more.

Blend in flour, curry powder, ginger, mace and pepper. Gradually stir in chicken broth and undrained mushrooms. Microwave (high setting) 20 minutes, or until sauce thickens, stirring every 4 minutes.

Stir in turkey and microwave (high setting) 4 minutes.

Stir a little of the hot mixture into sour cream. Then stir sour cream mixture back into baking dish. Microwave (high setting) 1 minute. (Do not boil.) Serve with rice and pass a selection of condiments. Makes 6 servings.

FISH FILLETS IN ALMOND BUTTER

⅓ c. sliced almonds
⅓ c. butter or regular
  margarine
2 tblsp. lemon juice
¼ tsp. dried dill

½ tsp. salt
1 lb. sole, halibut or perch
  fillets, fresh or frozen
  and thawed

Combine almonds and butter in 8″ square glass baking dish. Microwave (high setting) 5 to 6 minutes, or until almonds are golden brown.

Stir in lemon juice, dill and salt. Add fillets, spooning some of the sauce over fillets. Cover with waxed paper.

Microwave 3 to 5 minutes, or until fish begins to flake with a fork. Let stand 2 minutes. Makes 6 servings.

LOW-CAL FISH FLIP

2 (1-lb.) pkg. frozen fish fillets, thawed
⅔ c. thinly sliced onion
¼ lb. fresh mushrooms, sliced
½ c. chopped fresh tomato
¼ c. finely chopped green pepper

¼ c. chopped fresh parsley
3 tblsp. chopped pimiento
½ c. chicken broth
2 tblsp. lemon juice
¾ tsp. salt
⅛ tsp. pepper
⅛ tsp. dried dill

Cut each package of fish fillets into 3 sections and set aside.

Arrange onion in 12x8x2″ (2-qt.) glass baking dish. Top with mushrooms, tomato, green pepper, parsley and pimiento. Cover with plastic wrap, turning back one corner to let steam escape.

Microwave (high setting) 5 minutes. Arrange fillets on top of vegetables. Add remaining ingredients. Cover with plastic wrap, turning back one corner.

Microwave (medium setting) 15 to 18 minutes, or until fish begins to flake with a fork, rotating dish one-quarter turn every 5 minutes. Let stand 2 minutes. Arrange fish on serving platter and top with vegetables. Makes 6 servings.

STIR-FRIED SHRIMP WITH ASPARAGUS

1 lb. fresh asparagus,
bias-cut into ¼″ slices
1 clove garlic, minced
1 tblsp. sesame oil or
cooking oil
3 tblsp. water
1 lb. medium-size fresh
shrimp, shelled and
deveined

½ c. sliced green onions
½ c. chicken broth
3 tblsp. dry sherry
1 tblsp. soy sauce
¼ tsp. sugar
1 tblsp. cornstarch
Hot cooked rice

Combine asparagus, garlic and oil in 3-qt. glass casserole. Microwave (high setting) 2 minutes. Add water. Cover and microwave 1½ minutes. Stir. Microwave 1½ minutes more.

Add shrimp. Cover and microwave (high setting) 1 minute. Stir. Microwave 1 minute more. Stir in green onions and set aside.

Combine chicken broth, sherry, soy sauce, sugar and cornstarch in small glass bowl; stir to blend. Microwave (high setting) 1 minute. Stir. Microwave 1 minute more, or until sauce thickens. Stir sauce into shrimp mixture. Serve with rice. Makes 4 servings.

LINGUINI WITH WHITE CLAM SAUCE

2 (6½-oz.) cans chopped
  or minced clams
¼ c. butter or regular
  margarine
¼ c. cooking oil
3 cloves garlic, minced
¼ c. chopped fresh
  parsley

¼ tsp. dried oregano
  leaves
¼ tsp. dried basil leaves
⅛ tsp. pepper
8 oz. linguini, cooked and
  drained
Grated Parmesan cheese

Drain clams, reserving juice; set aside.

Place butter and oil in 1½-qt. glass casserole. Microwave (high setting) 1 minute, or until butter melts. Add garlic and microwave 1 minute more.

Stir parsley, oregano, basil, pepper and reserved clam juice into casserole. Cover and microwave (high setting) 4 minutes. Add clams and microwave 1 minute more or until hot.

Serve over hot cooked linguini and sprinkle with cheese. Makes 4 servings.

CHAPTER FOUR

VEGETABLES AND SIDE DISHES

HERBED CHERRY TOMATOES

1 pt. cherry tomatoes
3 tblsp. butter or regular
  margarine

1 clove garlic, minced
¼ tsp. dried oregano
  leaves

Wash and stem tomatoes.

Place butter in 1½-qt. glass casserole. Microwave (high setting) 1½ minutes or until melted. Add garlic and oregano. Microwave (high setting) 2 minutes.

Add tomatoes. Microwave (high setting) 1 minute. Stir gently. Microwave 1 minute more, or until tomato skins just begin to split. Makes 4 servings.

SPINACH-STUFFED MUSHROOMS

3 c. chopped, fresh
spinach, packed
1 lb. large fresh
mushrooms
¹/₃ c. sliced green onions
2 tblsp. butter or regular
margarine
¹/₄ c. chopped fresh
parsley

¹/₄ tsp. garlic salt
¹/₄ tsp. salt
¹/₈ tsp. pepper
¹/₈ tsp. ground nutmeg
1 (15-oz.) container ricotta cheese
¹/₄ c. grated Parmesan
cheese
Paprika

Rinse spinach in cold water; drain. Place spinach with water that clings to leaves in 1¹/₂-qt. glass casserole. Cover and microwave (high setting) 1¹/₂ minutes. Stir. Microwave 1 minute more or just until wilted. Let stand 2 minutes. Drain in colander. Press with spoon to squeeze out excess liquid. Set aside.

Remove stems from mushrooms and chop stems. Place in same 1¹/₂-qt. casserole. Add green onions and butter. Cover and microwave (high setting) 2 minutes. Stir. Microwave 2 minutes more.

Stir in parsley, garlic salt, salt, pepper, nutmeg and drained spinach. Cool slightly.

Stir in ricotta and Parmesan cheese. Spoon spinach mixture into mushroom caps. Sprinkle with paprika.

Arrange half of the mushrooms in a ring on microwave-safe plate lined with paper towels. Microwave (high setting) 2 to 4 minutes or until hot, rotating plate one-quarter turn after each minute. Repeat with remaining mushrooms. Makes 6 to 8 servings.

MARINATED GREEN BEANS

1 lb. fresh green beans
½ c. water
Italian Marinade (recipe
  follows)

⅓ c. sliced green onions
Lettuce leaves
2 tblsp. grated Parmesan
  cheese

Trim ends from green beans. French beans by slicing length-wise. Place green beans and water in 2-qt. glass casserole. Cover.

Microwave (high setting) 6 minutes. Stir. Microwave 6 minutes more, or until tender crisp. Drain well.

Prepare Italian Marinade.

Combine green beans and green onions in bowl. Pour Italian Marinade over vegetables, tossing to coat. Cover and refrigerate at least 3 hours.

To serve, arrange green beans on lettuce leaves. Sprinkle with cheese. Makes 4 servings.

Italian Marinade: Combine 6 tblsp. cooking oil, 2 tblsp. vinegar, ½ clove garlic (minced), ¼ tsp. dried basil leaves, ⅛ tsp. dry mustard and a dash of pepper in a jar. Cover and shake well.

ASPARAGUS WITH EGG SAUCE

2 lb. fresh asparagus, cut
  into 1½" lengths
¼ c. water
¼ c. chopped onion
2 tblsp. butter or regular
  margarine
2 tblsp. flour
¼ tsp. salt
¼ tsp. dry mustard
¼ tsp. Worcestershire
  sauce

Dash pepper
1 c. milk
½ (3-oz.) pkg. cream
  cheese, cubed
1 hard-cooked egg,
  chopped
2 tblsp. chopped fresh
  parsley
1 tblsp. chopped
  pimiento

Place asparagus and water in 2-qt. glass casserole. Cover and microwave (high setting) 5 minutes. Stir. Microwave 3 to 7 minutes more or until tender. Let stand covered.

Place onion and butter in 4-c. glass measuring cup. Microwave (high setting) 2 minutes or until tender. Blend in flour, salt, mustard, Worcestershire sauce and pepper.

Gradually stir in milk. Add cream cheese. Microwave (high setting) 2 minutes. Stir. Microwave 1 to 2 minutes more, or until sauce thickens, stirring after each minute. Stir in chopped egg, parsley and pimiento.

Drain asparagus and serve with egg sauce. Makes 6 servings.

CANDIED ACORN SQUASH

3 acorn squash (about
  2 lb.)
¼ c. butter or regular
  margarine

1 (8-oz.) can sliced
  pineapple in juice
1 c. packed brown sugar

Cut squash in half lengthwise. Remove seeds and stringy fibers and discard. Cut squash into 1" wedges. Arrange squash in 12x8x2" (2-qt.) glass baking dish. Cover tightly with plastic wrap. (Do not vent.)

Microwave (high setting) 5 minutes. Rearrange squash by moving outside pieces to center of dish. Cover tightly and microwave 4 minutes more or until squash is tender. Drain squash and return to baking dish. Cover to keep warm.

Place butter in 4-c. glass measuring cup. Microwave (high setting) 1 minute or until melted.

Drain pineapple, reserving juice. Cut pineapple slices in half; set aside. Stir reserved pineapple juice and brown sugar into butter. Microwave (high setting) 2 minutes. Stir. Microwave 2 minutes more.

Add pineapple to squash in baking dish. Spoon brown sugar mixture over squash and pineapple. Microwave (high setting) 1 minute or until hot. Makes 6 servings.

GOLDEN SQUASH BOATS

2 acorn squash (about
  1 lb. each)
Salt
Pepper
1 c. carrot strips (1½x³⁄₈")
2 medium onions, cut
  into eighths
½ tsp. salt

½ c. water
1 c. peas, fresh or frozen
  and thawed
3 tblsp. butter or regular
  margarine
3 tblsp. packed brown
  sugar

Cut squash in half lengthwise; remove seeds and stringy fibers and discard. Sprinkle with salt and pepper. Arrange in 12x8x2" (2-qt.) glass baking dish, cut side up. Cover tightly with plastic wrap. (Do not vent.)

Microwave (high setting) 8 minutes. Rotate dish one-quarter turn. Microwave 5 to 8 minutes more or until tender. Keep warm.

Place carrots and onions in 2-qt. glass casserole. Dissolve ½ tsp. salt in water; pour over vegetables. Cover and microwave (high setting) 5 minutes. Stir. Microwave 5 minutes more or until tender. Add peas. Microwave (high setting) 3 minutes. Drain in colander. Place butter in same 2-qt. casserole.

Microwave (high setting) 1 minute or until melted. Add drained carrots and onions. Sprinkle with brown sugar. Microwave (high setting) 2 minutes. Stir. Microwave 2 minutes more or until glazed. Spoon into squash halves. Makes 4 servings.

BROWN SUGAR-GLAZED ONIONS

1½ lb. small white onions
  (about 22)
½ tsp. salt
½ c. water
3 tblsp. butter or regular
  margarine

½ tsp. dry mustard
⅛ tsp. pepper
⅓ c. packed brown sugar

Slice off stem and root ends of onions and peel outer layers. Place onions in 1½-qt. casserole.

Dissolve salt in water; pour over onions. Cover and microwave (high setting) 7 minutes. Stir. Microwave 8 minutes more or until tender. Drain in colander. Place butter, mustard and pepper in same 1½-qt. casserole.

Microwave (high setting) 1 minute, or until butter melts; stir to blend. Add onions and sprinkle with brown sugar.

Microwave (high setting) 2 minutes. Turn onions and microwave 2 minutes more, or until onions are lightly glazed. Makes 4 servings.

POTATOES AU GRATIN

7 medium potatoes,
  pared and sliced
  (2½ lb.)
¾ c. very hot water
¾ c. chopped onion
¼ c. butter or regular
  margarine
¼ c. flour
1 tsp. dry mustard
1 tsp. salt

3 c. milk
1 tsp. Worcestershire
  sauce
2 c. shredded Cheddar
  cheese
½ c. saltine cracker
  crumbs
2 tblsp. butter or regular
  margarine, melted
Paprika

Arrange potatoes in 12x8x2" (2-qt.) glass baking dish. Pour hot water over potatoes. Cover with plastic wrap, turning back one corner to let steam escape.

Microwave (high setting) 30 minutes or until tender, stirring every 10 minutes. Drain potatoes in colander. Return potatoes to same 2-qt. baking dish and set aside.

Combine onion and ¼ c. butter in 2-qt. glass casserole. Cover and microwave (high setting) 2 minutes. Stir. Microwave 2 minutes more or until tender. Blend in flour, mustard and salt. Gradually stir in milk and Worcestershire sauce. Microwave (high setting) 3 minutes. Stir. Microwave 7 minutes more, or until sauce thickens, stirring after each minute. Add cheese; stir until melted.

Pour cheese sauce over potatoes. Combine cracker crumbs and 2 tblsp. melted butter. Sprinkle over potatoes, then sprinkle with paprika.

Microwave (high setting) 15 minutes or until hot and bubbly. Makes 6 servings.

HERBED SPINACH TIMBALES

1⅓ c. milk
2 tblsp. butter or regular
   margarine
2 (10-oz.) pkg. frozen
   chopped spinach,
   thawed and well
   drained

3 eggs, beaten
¼ tsp. dried tarragon
   leaves, crushed
¼ tsp. onion salt
¼ tsp. salt
⅛ tsp. pepper

Pour milk into 4-c. glass measuring cup. Microwave (high setting) 4 minutes or until scalded.

Combine hot milk and butter in bowl; stir until butter melts. Stir in remaining ingredients, mixing well. Spoon into 6 greased (6-oz.) glass custard cups.

Arrange 3 custard cups in a ring in microwave oven. Microwave (high setting) 1½ minutes. Rearrange timbales. Microwave 1½ minutes more, or until a knife inserted in center comes out clean. Loosen edges with spatula and invert onto serving platter. Repeat with remaining timbales. Makes 6 servings.

SPINACH-STUFFED TOMATOES

6 medium tomatoes
Salt
½ lb. fresh spinach
½ c. chopped fresh
mushrooms
2 tblsp. sliced green
onions
2 tblsp. butter or regular
margarine

1 tblsp. flour
¼ tsp. salt
⅛ tsp. ground nutmeg
6 tblsp. milk
1½ c. cooked rice
Blender Béarnaise Sauce
(recipe follows)

Cut slice from stem end of each tomato. Scoop out pulp and sprinkle inside of shells with salt. Invert on paper towels.

Rinse spinach and place in 2-qt. glass casserole. Cover and microwave (high setting) 3 minutes. Drain and chop.

Combine next 3 ingredients in same 1½-qt. casserole. Cover and microwave (high setting) 3 minutes. Blend in flour, ¼ tsp. salt and nutmeg. Stir in milk. Microwave (high setting) 3 minutes, or until mixture is very thick, stirring after each minute. Stir in spinach and rice.

Spoon into tomato shells. Place in 12x8x2" (2-qt.) glass baking dish. Cover with plastic wrap, turning back one corner. Microwave (high setting) 2 minutes. Rotate dish one-quarter turn. Microwave 2 to 3 minutes more or until hot. Prepare Blender Béarnaise Sauce and serve with tomatoes. Makes 6 servings.

Blender Béarnaise Sauce: Place 2 egg yolks, 1 tblsp. chopped onion, 1 tsp. dried tarragon leaves, ⅛ tsp. salt and 2 drops Tabasco sauce in blender jar. Cover and blend. Place ½ c. butter in glass bowl. Microwave (high setting) 1 minute. Add 1 tblsp. vinegar. Microwave 1 minute more. Slowly add butter mixture to yolk mixture in a steady stream; blend at high speed until thick.

TOMATO SCALLOP

½ c. chopped onion
½ c. chopped green
   pepper
¼ c. butter or regular
   margarine
2 c. soft bread crumbs
⅓ c. grated Romano
   cheese

¾ tsp. salt
⅛ tsp. pepper
4 medium tomatoes,
   peeled and sliced
   (1½ lb.)
Grated Romano cheese

Combine onion, green pepper and butter in glass bowl. Cover with plastic wrap, turning back one corner to let steam escape.

Microwave (high setting) 4 minutes or until tender. Stir in bread crumbs, ⅓ c. cheese, salt and pepper.

Arrange one-third of the tomatoes in 10x6x2" (1½-qt.) glass baking dish. Sprinkle with half of the bread crumb mixture. Repeat layers, ending with tomatoes.

Microwave (high setting) 15 minutes, or until tomatoes are tender, rotating dish one-quarter turn every 5 minutes. Sprinkle with cheese. Makes 6 servings.

✓ ZUCCHINI AND TOMATO PARMESAN

1½ c. chopped green
  pepper
1 c. chopped onion
1 clove garlic, minced
2 tblsp. cooking oil
4½ c. sliced zucchini
  (1½ lb.)

5 medium tomatoes,
  chopped
2 tsp. salt
⅛ tsp. pepper
2 tsp. cornstarch
2 tblsp. water
Grated Parmesan cheese

Combine green pepper, onion, garlic and oil in 3-qt. glass casserole. Cover and microwave (high setting) 3 minutes. Stir. Microwave 3 minutes more or until tender.

Stir in zucchini, tomatoes, salt and pepper. Cover and microwave (high setting) 8 minutes. Stir. Microwave 7 minutes. Remove cover. Microwave 5 minutes more.

Combine cornstarch and water in bowl; stir to blend. Stir cornstarch mixture into vegetables. Microwave (high setting) 2 minutes, or until mixture thickens. Cover and let stand 5 minutes. Serve with grated Parmesan cheese. Makes 4 to 6 servings.

VEGETABLE-STUFFED ZUCCHINI

3 zucchini (about ½ lb.
  each)
4 strips bacon, diced
½ c. chopped onion
2 medium tomatoes,
  chopped

1 c. cooked whole-kernel
  corn
¼ tsp. salt
Dash of pepper
½ c. grated Parmesan
  cheese

Cut zucchini in half lengthwise. Scoop out seeds and pulp to form ¼" thick shell. Set zucchini shells aside. If desired, reserve pulp for later use in soup.

Place bacon in 1½-qt. glass casserole. Cover and microwave (high setting) 3 to 4 minutes or until crisp. Remove bacon with slotted spoon and drain on paper towels.

Add onion to drippings in casserole. Cover and microwave (high setting) 4 minutes or until tender. Stir in tomatoes, corn, salt and pepper. Cover and microwave (high setting) 3 minutes. Stir. Microwave 3 minutes more. Drain liquid from mixture. Stir in bacon.

Spoon tomato mixture into zucchini shells and place in 12x8x2" (2-qt.) glass baking dish. Sprinkle with cheese. Cover with waxed paper.

Microwave (high setting) 5 minutes. Rotate dish one-quarter turn. Microwave 5 minutes more or until hot. Makes 6 servings.

MIXED VEGETABLE PLATTER

1½ lb. fresh broccoli
½ medium head
  cauliflower
¼ lb. fresh mushrooms,
  sliced ¼" thick

1 c. thinly sliced, pared
  carrots
2 tblsp. water
Italian Vinaigrette (recipe
  follows)

Cut tough end from lower stalk of broccoli and discard. Cut broccoli into 1" flowerets, leaving stems 2" long. Peel stems. Cut cauliflower into 1" flowerets.

Arrange mushrooms in a ring around the edge of 12" round, microwave-safe plate. Then arrange a ring of broccoli and a ring of cauliflower. Place carrots in center. Sprinkle with water. Cover tightly with plastic wrap. (Do not vent.)

Microwave (high setting) 3 minutes. Rotate plate one-quarter turn. Microwave 3 minutes more, or until vegetables are tender-crisp. Let stand 2 minutes; pour off liquid. Prepare Italian Vinaigrette. Serve Italian Vinaigrette with warm vegetables; or pour Italian Vinaigrette over vegetables, refrigerate, and serve chilled. Makes 6 servings.

Italian Vinaigrette: Combine ¾ c. cooking oil, ⅓ c. vinegar, 1 clove garlic (quartered), 1 tblsp. chopped onion, ½ tsp. salt, ⅛ tsp. dried rosemary leaves, ⅛ tsp. dried basil leaves, ⅛ tsp. dried oregano leaves and dash cayenne pepper in blender jar. Cover and blend until smooth.

ORIENTAL STIR-FRIED VEGETABLES

1½ lb. fresh broccoli
1 c. chicken broth
1 tblsp. sesame oil or
cooking oil
1 clove garlic, minced
½ tsp. salt
¼ lb. fresh mushrooms,
sliced
1 (16-oz.) can bean
sprouts, drained

1 (8-oz.) can water chestnuts, drained and sliced
1 (6-oz.) pkg. frozen pea
pods, thawed
3 tsp. cornstarch
1 tsp. sugar
⅛ tsp. ground ginger
1 tblsp. soy sauce
1 tblsp. toasted sesame
seeds

Cut tough end from lower stalk of broccoli and discard. Remove flowerets and cut in half. Cut stalks into 2x¼" strips.

Place broccoli, ½ c. of the chicken broth, sesame oil, garlic and salt in 3-qt. glass casserole. Cover and microwave (high setting) 4 minutes. Stir. Microwave 4 minutes more.

Stir in mushrooms. Cover and microwave (high setting) 2 minutes.

Stir in bean sprouts, water chestnuts and pea pods. Cover and microwave (high setting) 2 minutes. Drain vegetables, reserving liquid. Place reserved liquid in 2-c. glass measuring cup.

Combine cornstarch, sugar, ginger, soy sauce and remaining ½ c. chicken broth in bowl; stir to blend. Stir cornstarch mixture into reserved vegetable liquid. Microwave (high setting) 4 minutes, or until mixture thickens, stirring after each minute. Stir cornstarch mixture into vegetable mixture. Sprinkle with sesame seeds. Makes 4 to 6 servings.

STIR-FRIED CARROTS AND BROCCOLI

1¼ lb. fresh broccoli	1 tblsp. soy sauce
2 c. bias-cut, pared carrots (⅛″ slices)	½ tsp. sugar
2 tblsp. cooking oil	½ tsp. salt
1 c. chicken broth	1 tblsp. cornstarch
1 clove garlic, minced	2 tblsp. toasted sliced almonds

Cut tough end from lower stalk of broccoli and discard. Remove flowerets and cut larger ones in half. Cut stalks into 2½x⅛″ strips. Place broccoli and carrots in 3-qt. glass casserole. Sprinkle with oil. Cover and microwave (high setting) 2 minutes. Stir. Microwave 2 minutes more.

Stir in ¾ c. of the chicken broth, garlic, soy sauce, sugar and salt. Cover and microwave (high setting) 4 minutes. Stir. Microwave 3 minutes more, or until vegetables are tender-crisp. Remove vegetables with slotted spoon; keep warm.

Combine cornstarch and remaining ¼ c. chicken broth in bowl; stir to blend. Add cornstarch mixture to liquid in casserole. Microwave (high setting) 1 minute. Stir. Microwave 1 minute more, or until mixture thickens. Stir vegetables back into broth mixture. Garnish with toasted almonds. Makes 6 servings.

BACON-FRIED RICE

½ lb. bacon, diced
4 eggs, beaten
⅛ tsp. pepper
¾ c. chopped onion
¾ c. chopped green
  pepper
¼ lb. fresh mushrooms,
  sliced

3 c. cold cooked rice
2 tblsp. chopped fresh
  parsley
½ tsp. salt
Soy sauce

Place bacon in 2-qt. glass casserole. Cover and microwave (high setting) 4 minutes. Stir. Microwave 4 minutes more or until crisp. Remove with a slotted spoon and drain on paper towels. Pour bacon drippings into a small bowl.

Place 1 tblsp. of the drippings in 9″ glass pie plate. Add eggs and pepper to pie plate. Microwave (medium setting) 3 to 4 minutes. Lift edge so uncooked portion flows underneath. Microwave 2 to 4 minutes more or until almost set. Set aside.

Return 1 more tblsp. of the drippings to 2-qt. glass casserole. Add onion, green pepper and mushrooms. Cover and microwave (high setting) 5 minutes or until tender.

Stir in rice, parsley, salt and bacon. Cover and microwave (high setting) 1 minute. Stir. Microwave 1 minute more or until hot.

Cut eggs into small pieces and stir into casserole. Serve with soy sauce. Makes 6 servings.

GOLDEN RICE PILAF

1 c. chopped onion
1 c. shredded, pared
  carrots
1/2 c. sliced celery
1/2 c. chopped green
  pepper
2 cloves garlic, minced
1/2 c. butter or regular
  margarine

1 1/2 c. uncooked regular
  rice
1 3/4 c. chicken broth
1 c. very hot water
1/4 c. chopped fresh
  parsley
1/2 tsp. salt
1/8 tsp. pepper

Place onion, carrots, celery, green pepper, garlic and 2 tblsp. of the butter in 2-qt. glass casserole. Cover and microwave (high setting) 3 minutes. Stir. Microwave 3 minutes more or until tender. Remove vegetables and set aside. Place remaining 6 tblsp. butter and rice in same 2-qt. casserole.

Cover and microwave (high setting) 3 minutes. Stir. Microwave 2 minutes more, or until rice is browned and most of the butter has been absorbed. Stir in chicken broth, hot water, parsley, salt, pepper and onion mixture. Cover.

Microwave (high setting) 10 minutes. Stir. Microwave 8 minutes more, or until rice is tender. Let stand, covered, 5 minutes. Fluff with fork before serving. Makes 8 servings.

CREAMY NOODLES AU GRATIN

1 c. shredded Cheddar
  cheese
1 c. shredded Swiss
  cheese
8 oz. wide egg noodles,
  cooked and drained
3 tblsp. butter or regular
  margarine

½ tsp. salt
⅛ tsp. pepper
1 c. dairy sour cream
½ c. milk
1½ c. soft bread crumbs
2 tblsp. butter or regular
  margarine, melted

Toss together Cheddar and Swiss cheese.

Place one-third of the noodles in greased 1½-qt. glass casserole. Dot with 1 tblsp. of the butter. Top with layers of one-third of the cheese, salt, pepper and sour cream. Repeat layers twice. Pour milk over all.

Combine bread crumbs and 2 tblsp. melted butter in bowl; toss to mix. Sprinkle over casserole.

Microwave (high setting) 3 minutes. Rotate dish one-quarter turn. Microwave 3 minutes more or until hot and bubbly. Makes 8 servings.

GOLDEN PEAR RELISH

6 ripe pears (about 2 lb.)
1 c. sugar
⅔ c. white vinegar
3 tblsp. prepared yellow
   mustard

2 tsp. salt
⅔ c. chopped onion
⅓ c. diced green pepper
2 tblsp. raisins
1 tblsp. diced pimiento

Pare and cut pears lengthwise into eighths. Remove cores and discard.

Combine sugar, vinegar, mustard and salt in 2-qt. glass casserole. Microwave (high setting) 3 minutes, or until mixture comes to a boil.

Add pears, onion, green pepper, raisins and pimiento. Microwave (high setting) 10 minutes, or until pears are tender and mustard-colored. Refrigerate in tightly covered container. Serve chilled. Makes 4 cups.

SUGAR 'N' SPICE APPLESAUCE

8 c. coarsely chopped,	**⅓ c. packed brown sugar**
pared cooking apples	**½ tsp. ground cinnamon**
2 tblsp. water	**⅛ tsp. ground mace**

Combine apples and water in 3-qt. glass casserole. Cover.

Microwave (high setting) 17 minutes, or until apples are very tender, stirring every 5 minutes.

Stir in brown sugar, cinnamon and mace. Cover and microwave (high setting) 2 minutes.

Mash mixture lightly with a fork for chunky applesauce. For smooth applesauce, force mixture through a food mill or purée in a blender or food processor.

Serve warm or chilled. Makes about 4 c.

HOT SPICED FRUIT

1 (29-oz.) can pear halves, drained
1 (20-oz.) can sliced pineapple, drained
1 (16-oz.) can apricot halves, drained
1 (11-oz.) can mandarin orange segments, drained

½ c. butter or regular margarine
1 c. packed brown sugar
1 tsp. ground cinnamon
⅛ tsp. ground cloves

Pat fruit dry with paper towels and arrange in 12x8x2" (2-qt.) glass baking dish.

Place butter in small glass bowl and microwave (high setting) 1 minute or until melted. Stir in brown sugar, cinnamon and cloves. Spoon over fruit.

Microwave (high setting) 5 minutes. Rotate dish one-quarter turn and microwave 5 minutes more or until bubbly. Makes 8 servings.

PECAN STUFFING

2 c. sliced celery	Water
1 c. chopped onion	1 (13¾-oz.) can chicken
½ c. butter or regular	broth
margarine	2 tsp. rubbed sage
¼ c. chopped fresh	⅛ tsp. pepper
parsley	1 c. pecan halves
1 (4-oz.) can sliced	8 c. toasted white bread
mushrooms	cubes (³/₈″)

Place celery, onion and butter in 3-qt. glass casserole. Cover and microwave (high setting) 4 minutes. Stir. Microwave 4 minutes more or until tender. Stir in parsley. Microwave 1 minute more.

Drain mushrooms, reserving liquid. Add enough water to liquid to make ⅔ c. Stir mushrooms, ⅔ c. liquid, chicken broth, sage and pepper into casserole.

Microwave (high setting) 4 minutes. Stir. Microwave 3 minutes more or until hot.

Stir in pecan halves and toasted bread cubes. Cover and let stand 10 minutes before serving. Makes 8 servings.

CHAPTER FIVE

BREADS AND DESSERTS

CORN MEAL BRAN MUFFINS

1¼ c. milk	½ c. packed dark brown
1¼ c. all-bran cereal	sugar
¾ c. stirred whole-wheat	3 tsp. baking powder
flour	½ tsp. salt
½ c. sifted flour (all-	1 egg
purpose)	⅓ c. cooking oil
⅓ c. yellow corn meal	Wheat germ

Pour milk over bran cereal in small bowl. Let stand 5 minutes.

Meanwhile, stir together whole-wheat flour, all-purpose flour, corn meal, brown sugar, baking powder and salt in another bowl; set aside.

Add egg and oil to cereal mixture; beat well. Add all at once to dry ingredients, stirring just until moistened.

Place two paper muffin-pan liners in each of 7 (6-oz.) glass custard cups. Spoon half of the batter into lined cups, filling half full. Sprinkle with wheat germ. Arrange cups in a ring in microwave oven. Microwave (high setting) 1½ minutes. Rearrange cups and microwave 1½ to 2 minutes more, or until a wooden pick inserted in center of muffin comes out clean.

Remove muffins from cups. Repeat with remaining batter. Serve warm. Makes 14 muffins.

OLD-FASHIONED BLUEBERRY MUFFINS

1¾ c. sifted flour
¼ c. sugar
3 tsp. baking powder
½ tsp. salt
½ c. butter or regular
   margarine

1 egg
¾ c. milk
½ c. fresh blueberries
⅔ c. sugar
2 tsp. ground cinnamon

Sift together flour, ¼ c. sugar, baking powder and salt into bowl. Cut in butter until mixture resembles corn meal, using a pastry blender.

Combine egg and milk; beat well. Add all at once to flour mixture, stirring just until moistened. Gently stir in blueberries.

Place two paper muffin-pan liners in each of 6 (6-oz.) glass custard cups. Spoon 2 tblsp. of the batter into each lined cup. Combine ⅔ c. sugar and cinnamon; mix well. Sprinkle some of the sugar-cinnamon mixture over each muffin. Arrange cups in a ring in 10″ glass pie plate. Microwave (high setting) 1 minute. Rearrange cups and microwave 1½ minutes more, or until a wooden pick inserted in center of muffin comes out clean. Remove muffins from cups. Repeat twice more with remaining batter and topping. Serve warm. Makes 18 muffins.

CHEESY BACON CORN MUFFINS

8 strips bacon, diced	**2 eggs**
¼ c. chopped onion	**1 c. milk**
1¼ c. sifted flour	**3 tblsp. butter or regular**
¾ c. yellow corn meal	**margarine, melted**
½ c. sugar	**½ c. shredded Cheddar**
3 tsp. baking powder	**cheese**
1 tsp. salt	

Combine bacon and onion in 1-qt. glass casserole. Cover with paper towel. Microwave (high setting) 3 minutes. Stir. Microwave 2 minutes more, or until bacon is crisp. Drain bacon and onion on paper towels.

Sift together flour, corn meal, sugar, baking powder and salt in bowl; set aside.

Combine eggs, milk and butter in another bowl; beat well. Add all at once to dry ingredients, stirring just until moistened. Stir in bacon-onion mixture and cheese.

Place two paper muffin-pan liners in each of 7 (6-oz.) glass custard cups. Spoon half of the batter into lined cups, filling half full. Arrange cups in a ring in microwave oven. Microwave (high setting) 1½ minutes. Rearrange cups and microwave 1½ minutes more, or until a wooden pick inserted in center of muffin comes out clean. Remove muffins from cups. Repeat with remaining batter. Serve warm. Makes 14 muffins.

OATMEAL-RAISIN MUFFINS

1 c. sifted flour
3 tsp. baking powder
1 tsp. salt
½ tsp. ground cinnamon
¼ tsp. ground nutmeg
1 c. quick-cooking oats
½ c. raisins
¾ c. milk
½ c. cooking oil

⅓ c. packed brown sugar
1 egg
6 tblsp. flour
3 tblsp. packed brown
   sugar
1½ tsp. ground cinnamon
3 tblsp. butter or regular
   margarine

Sift together 1 c. flour, baking powder, salt, ½ tsp. cinnamon and nutmeg in bowl; set aside.

Combine oats, raisins, milk, oil, ⅓ c. brown sugar and egg in bowl; beat well. Add all at once to dry ingredients, stirring just until moistened.

Place two paper muffin-pan liners in each of 6 (6-oz.) glass custard cups. Spoon half of the batter into lined cups, filling two-thirds full. Combine 6 tblsp. flour, 3 tblsp. brown sugar and 1½ tsp. cinnamon in small bowl. Cut in butter until crumbs form, using a pastry blender. Sprinkle half of the crumb mixture over muffins. Arrange cups in a ring in microwave oven. Microwave (high setting) 1 minute. Rearrange cups and microwave 1¾ minutes more, or until a wooden pick inserted in center of muffin comes out clean. Remove muffins from cups. Repeat with remaining batter and crumb mixture. Serve warm. Makes 12 muffins.

ORANGE CRUMB MUFFINS

1½ c. sifted flour	½ c. cooking oil
¼ c. sugar	½ c. milk
¼ c. packed brown sugar	1 tsp. grated orange rind
2 tsp. baking powder	Crumb Topping (recipe
½ tsp. salt	follows)
½ tsp. ground cinnamon	Vanilla Icing (recipe
1 egg	follows)

Stir together flour, sugar, brown sugar, baking powder, salt and cinnamon in bowl; set aside.

Combine egg, oil, milk and orange rind in small bowl; beat well. Add all at once to dry ingredients, stirring just until moistened.

Place two paper muffin-pan liners in each of 7 (6-oz.) glass custard cups. Spoon half of the batter into lined cups, filling half full. Prepare Crumb Topping and sprinkle half of the topping over muffins. Arrange cups in a ring in microwave oven. Microwave (high setting) 1½ minutes. Rearrange cups and microwave 1½ minutes more, or until a wooden pick inserted in center of muffin comes out clean. Remove muffins from cups. Repeat with remaining batter and topping.

Prepare Vanilla Icing and drizzle over hot muffins. Serve warm. Makes 14 muffins.

Crumb Topping: Combine ½ c. chopped pecans, ½ c. packed brown sugar, ¼ c. flour, ¼ tsp. ground cinnamon and 2 tblsp. butter or regular margarine (melted) in bowl. Mix until crumbly.

Vanilla Icing: Combine ¾ c. sifted confectioners' sugar, 1 tblsp. milk and ½ tsp. vanilla in bowl. Stir until smooth.

CRANBERRY CRUNCH MUFFINS

2 c. sifted flour
¼ c. sugar
3 tsp. baking powder
½ tsp. salt
1 egg
¼ c. cooking oil
¾ c. milk

¼ c. orange juice
½ tsp. grated orange rind
1 c. chopped cranberries,
  fresh or frozen
¼ c. chopped walnuts
¼ c. packed brown sugar
½ tsp. ground cinnamon

Sift together flour, sugar, baking powder and salt into bowl; set aside.

Combine egg, oil, milk, orange juice and orange rind in small bowl; beat well. Add all at once to dry ingredients, stirring just until moistened. Gently stir in cranberries.

Place two paper muffin-pan liners in each of 7 (6-oz.) glass custard cups. Spoon half of the batter into lined cups. Combine walnuts, brown sugar and cinnamon in bowl; mix well. Sprinkle half of the walnut mixture over muffins. Arrange cups in a ring in microwave oven. Microwave (high setting) 1½ minutes. Rearrange cups and microwave 1½ minutes more, or until a wooden pick inserted in center of muffin comes out clean. Remove muffins from cups. Repeat with remaining batter and topping. Serve warm. Makes 14 muffins.

CARROT-WALNUT BREAD

1½ c. sifted flour
1 tsp. baking soda
½ tsp. ground cinnamon
¼ tsp. ground nutmeg
¼ tsp. salt
1 c. sugar
¾ c. cooking oil

2 eggs
1½ c. shredded, pared
  carrots
½ c. finely chopped
  walnuts
Confectioners' sugar

Sift together flour, baking soda, cinnamon, nutmeg and salt; set aside.

Combine sugar, oil and eggs in bowl. Beat 2 minutes, using an electric mixer at medium speed. Add dry ingredients, stirring just until moistened. Stir in carrots and walnuts. Pour batter into greased 8x4x2″ glass loaf dish. Place dish in microwave oven on an inverted saucer.

Microwave (medium setting) 15 minutes, rotating dish one-quarter turn every 4 minutes. Cool in dish directly on counter.

Remove from dish and sprinkle with confectioners' sugar. Makes 1 loaf.

ZUCCHINI NUT BREAD

2 c. sifted flour	1⅓ c. sugar
1 tsp. ground cinnamon	⅔ c. cooking oil
½ tsp. baking soda	2 tsp. vanilla
½ tsp. salt	1⅓ c. shredded zucchini
¼ tsp. baking powder	½ c. chopped pecans
2 eggs	Confectioners' sugar

Sift together flour, cinnamon, baking soda, salt and baking powder; set aside.

Beat eggs in bowl until blended, using an electric mixer at medium speed. Gradually add sugar and oil, mixing well after each addition. Blend in vanilla.

Add dry ingredients all at once, using an electric mixer at low speed. Stir in zucchini and pecans. Pour batter into greased 8″ square glass baking dish. Place dish in microwave oven on an inverted saucer.

Microwave (medium setting) 15 minutes, or until a wooden pick inserted in center comes out clean, rotating dish one-quarter turn every 4 minutes. Cool in dish directly on counter. Sprinkle with confectioners' sugar. Makes 1 loaf.

ORANGE-RAISIN CAKE

½ thin-skinned orange	¼ c. shortening
½ c. raisins	½ c. sugar
1 c. sifted flour	1 egg
½ tsp. baking soda	½ c. milk
½ tsp. baking powder	Fluffy Orange Frosting
¼ tsp. salt	(recipe follows)

Cut orange into pieces. Remove seeds but do not peel. Grind orange and raisins in food grinder, using a fine blade. Set aside.

Sift together flour, baking soda, baking powder and salt. Set aside.

Cream together shortening and sugar in bowl until light and fluffy, using an electric mixer at medium speed. Add egg; beat well.

Add dry ingredients alternately with milk to creamed mixture, beating well after each addition. Stir in orange-raisin mixture. Pour batter into greased 8" square glass baking dish. Place in microwave oven on an inverted saucer.

Microwave (medium setting) 3 minutes. Rotate dish one-quarter turn. Microwave (high setting) 2 to 3 minutes more, or until top springs back when touched with finger in several places, rotating dish one-quarter turn and checking for doneness every 30 seconds. Cool in dish directly on counter.

Prepare Fluffy Orange Frosting and frost cake. Makes 9 servings.

Fluffy Orange Frosting: Combine 1½ c. sifted confectioners' sugar, ¼ c. soft butter or regular margarine, ½ tsp. grated orange rind, 4 tsp. orange juice and ½ tsp. vanilla in bowl; beat until smooth, using an electric mixer at medium speed.

ELEGANT STRAWBERRY TORTE

3 c. sifted cake flour
1½ c. packed brown sugar
½ tsp. salt
1 c. butter or regular
   margarine
1 egg, beaten
1 c. sour milk*

1 tsp. baking soda
½ c. chopped pecans
1 pt. heavy cream,
   whipped and sweetened
1 pt. fresh strawberries,
   sliced

Combine cake flour, brown sugar and salt in bowl. Cut in butter until crumbly, using a pastry blender. Remove 1 c. of crumb mixture and set aside.

Combine egg, sour milk and baking soda in bowl; blend well. Stir egg mixture into remaining crumb mixture. Pour batter into 2 greased and waxed paper-lined 8″ round glass baking dishes. Sprinkle each with reserved 1 c. crumb mixture and pecans.

Microwave (medium setting) one layer at a time, 3 minutes. Rotate dish one-quarter turn. Microwave (high setting) 3 minutes, or until top springs back when touched with finger. (Moist spots on surface will evaporate as cake cools.) Let stand directly on counter 10 minutes. Remove from dish; cool on rack.

To assemble, place one layer on cake plate, crumb side up. Spread with half of the whipped cream. Top with sliced strawberries, reserving 12 slices. Top with second layer, crumb side up. Spoon remaining whipped cream in 12 puffs around edge of cake. Top each puff with one strawberry slice. Refrigerate until serving time. Makes 12 servings.

*To sour milk, place 1 tblsp. vinegar in measuring cup and add enough milk to make 1 c.

CHOCOLATE SURPRISE CUPCAKES

2 (3-oz.) pkg. cream
    cheese, softened
1 egg
⅓ c. sugar
⅛ tsp. salt
1 (6-oz.) pkg. semisweet
    chocolate pieces
1½ c. sifted flour
1 c. sugar

¼ c. baking cocoa
1 tsp. baking soda
½ tsp. salt
1 c. water
⅓ c. cooking oil
1 tblsp. vinegar
1 tsp. vanilla
2 tblsp. sugar
½ c. chopped walnuts

Beat cream cheese in bowl until smooth, using an electric mixer at medium speed. Add egg, ⅓ c. sugar and ⅛ tsp. salt. Beat until blended. Stir in chocolate pieces; set aside.

Sift together flour, 1 c. sugar, cocoa, baking soda and ½ tsp. salt into mixing bowl. Set aside.

Combine water, oil, vinegar and vanilla in another small bowl; mix well. Add to dry ingredients and beat until well blended, using an electric mixer at medium speed.

Place two paper muffin-pan liners in each of 6 (6-oz.) glass custard cups. Spoon half of the batter into lined cups, filling one-third full. Top each with a heaping teaspoonful of cream cheese mixture. Combine 2 tblsp. sugar and walnuts in bowl; mix well. Sprinkle 1 tsp. of the sugar-walnut mixture over cupcakes. Arrange cups in ring in microwave oven. Microwave (high setting) 1 minute. Rearrange cups and microwave 1 minute more, or until a wooden pick inserted in center of cupcake comes out clean. Remove cupcakes from cups; cool on rack. Repeat with remaining batter, cream cheese mixture and topping. Makes 12 cupcakes.

CHOCOLATE SNOW COOKIES

1¾ c. sifted flour	½ c. sugar
½ c. baking cocoa	½ tsp. vanilla
⅛ tsp. salt	1 c. chopped walnuts
¾ c. butter or regular margarine	Confectioners' sugar

Sift together flour, cocoa and salt; set aside.

Cream together butter and sugar in bowl until light and fluffy, using an electric mixer at medium speed. Blend in vanilla.

Gradually stir dry ingredients into creamed mixture, blending well. Stir in walnuts. Shape dough into (1") balls.

Arrange 9 balls in a ring on 10" round of cardboard covered with waxed paper. Place cardboard on an inverted saucer in microwave oven. Microwave (high setting) 1 minute. Rotate cardboard one-quarter turn. Microwave 1 minute more or until cookies are set. Let stand 2 minutes. Slide waxed paper and cookies from cardboard to counter. Cool completely on counter. Repeat with remaining dough.

When cool, sprinkle cookies with confectioners' sugar. Makes 3 dozen cookies.

PEANUT BUTTER CHIP BROWNIES

1⅓ c. sifted flour
⅛ tsp. baking soda
½ c. butter or regular
  margarine
1 c. sugar
2 eggs
1 tsp. vanilla
¾ c. chocolate-flavored
  syrup

1 c. peanut butter-
  flavored chips (6 oz.)
Peanut Butter Glaze
  (recipe follows)
¼ c. chopped peanuts
½ (1-oz.) square unsweet-
  ened chocolate, melted
  and cooled

Sift together flour and baking soda; set aside.

Cream together butter and sugar in bowl until light and fluffy, using an electric mixer at medium speed. Add eggs, one at a time, beating well after each addition. Blend in vanilla.

Add dry ingredients alternately with chocolate syrup to creamed mixture, beating well after each addition. Stir in chips. Spread mixture in 2 greased 8″ square glass baking dishes.

Microwave (high setting), one dish at a time, 2 minutes. Rotate dish one-quarter turn. Microwave 2½ minutes more, or until a wooden pick inserted in center comes out clean. Cool in dish directly on counter.

Prepare Peanut Butter Glaze. Immediately pour glaze over brownies and spread quickly. Sprinkle with peanuts and drizzle with chocolate. Cut into 2″ squares. Makes 32 squares.

Peanut Butter Glaze: Combine ⅓ c. sugar, ¼ c. evaporated milk and 2 tablespoons butter or regular margarine in 4-c. glass measuring cup. Microwave (high setting) 1 to 2 minutes, or until mixture boils, stirring after each minute. Add 1 c. peanut butter-flavored chips (6 oz.), stirring until melted. (If chips do not melt, microwave ½ minute more.) Blend in 1 tsp. vanilla.

PEANUT BUTTER-GRANOLA SQUARES

¾ c. sifted flour
¼ tsp. baking soda
¼ tsp. salt
¼ tsp. ground cinnamon
¼ c. butter or regular
  margarine
½ c. packed brown sugar
1 c. peanut butter-
  flavored chips (6 oz.)

1 egg
2 tblsp. milk
½ tsp. vanilla
½ c. natural granola
½ c. golden raisins
½ c. flaked coconut
½ c. peanuts

Sift together flour, baking soda, salt and cinnamon; set aside.

Combine butter and brown sugar in 2-qt. glass bowl. Micro-wave (high setting) 1 minute. Stir. Microwave 1 minute more or until butter melts and mixture begins to bubble. Add peanut butter chips, stirring until melted. Cool to lukewarm.

Add egg to peanut butter chip mixture. Beat until smooth, us-ing a wooden spoon. Blend in milk and vanilla. Gradually stir in dry ingredients. Stir in granola, raisins, coconut and peanuts. Spread mixture in greased 8" square glass baking dish. Place in microwave oven on an inverted saucer.

Microwave (high setting) 5 minutes, or until a wooden pick in-serted in center comes out clean, rotating dish one-quarter turn every 2 minutes. Cool in dish directly on counter. Cut into 2" squares. Makes 16 squares.

LEMON SQUARES

1 c. sifted flour
¼ c. sifted confectioners'
   sugar
⅓ c. butter or regular
   margarine
2 eggs

1 c. sugar
3 tblsp. lemon juice
1 tsp. grated lemon rind
1 tblsp. flour
½ tsp. baking powder
Confectioners' sugar

Combine 1 c. flour and ¼ c. confectioners' sugar in bowl. Cut in butter until mixture is crumbly, using a pastry blender. Press mixture into bottom and ½" up sides of 8" square glass baking dish.

Microwave (high setting) 2 minutes. Rotate dish one-quarter turn. Microwave 2 minutes more or until set.

Combine eggs, sugar, lemon juice, lemon rind, 1 tblsp. flour and baking powder in bowl. Beat until blended, using an electric mixer at medium speed. Pour over crust.

Microwave (high setting) 3½ minutes, or until top is bubbly, rotating dish one-quarter turn after each minute. Cool in dish directly on counter. When cool, sprinkle with confectioners' sugar and cut into 2" squares. Makes 16 squares.

ORANGE-FROSTED COCONUT BARS

1 c. sifted flour
¼ c. packed brown sugar
⅓ c. butter or regular
  margarine
2 eggs
1 c. packed brown sugar
2 tblsp. flour
½ tsp. baking powder

¼ tsp. salt
1 tsp. vanilla
1 c. chopped walnuts
½ c. flaked coconut
1 orange
Orange Icing (recipe
  follows)

Combine 1 c. flour and ¼ c. brown sugar in bowl. Cut in butter until mixture is crumbly, using a pastry blender. Press into bottom of 12x8x2" (2-qt.) glass baking dish.

Microwave (high setting) 2 minutes. Rotate dish one-quarter turn. Microwave 2 minutes more. Let stand directly on counter 5 minutes.

Meanwhile, beat eggs slightly in bowl, using an electric mixer at medium speed. Add 1 c. brown sugar, 2 tblsp. flour, baking powder, salt and vanilla; beat until blended. Stir in walnuts and coconut. Pour over baked layer.

Microwave (high setting) 4½ minutes or until set, rotating dish one-quarter turn every 2 minutes. Cool in dish directly on counter.

Peel a thin layer of skin from orange, using a vegetable peeler. Slice into thin strips. Set aside. Prepare Orange Icing and frost bars. Sprinkle with slivered orange rind. Cut into 3x1" bars. Makes 32 bars.

Orange Icing: Combine 1 c. sifted confectioners' sugar, 3½ tsp. orange juice and 1 tsp. lemon juice in bowl. Beat until smooth, using a spoon.

ORANGE-RHUBARB PIE

Orange Pastry (recipe follows)
Sugar
5 c. cut-up fresh rhubarb (¾ " lengths)

1¼ c. sugar
¼ c. flour
2 tsp. grated orange rind

Prepare Orange Pastry. Remove one-third of the pastry and set aside. Roll out remaining pastry on floured surface to 13" circle. Fit into 9" glass pie plate. Trim edge to 1" beyond rim of pie plate. Fold under edge of crust and form a ridge. Flute edge. Prick surface of shell with a fork. Microwave (high setting) 3 minutes. Rotate plate one-half turn. Microwave 3 minutes more, or until dry and opaque. (Cover any brown spots as they appear with small pieces of aluminum foil.) Cool on rack.

Roll out reserved pastry to 8" circle. Cut into 8 wedges. Sprinkle each with sugar. Place wedges on waxed paper. Microwave (high setting) 2 to 4 minutes, or until dry and opaque, rotating one-quarter turn after each minute. Cool on rack.

Combine rhubarb, 1¼ c. sugar, flour and orange rind in bowl; mix well. Arrange rhubarb mixture in pie shell. Place pie on a sheet of waxed paper in bottom of microwave oven.

Microwave (high setting) 6 minutes. Rotate plate one-quarter turn. Microwave 3 minutes more. Rotate plate one-quarter turn. Microwave 3 minutes more, or until bubbly. Cool on rack. To serve, arrange pastry wedges on top of pie. Makes 6 to 8 servings.

Orange Pastry: Combine 1¾ c. sifted flour, ¾ tsp. salt and ½ tsp. grated orange rind in bowl. Cut in ⅔ c. regular margarine until coarse crumbs form, using a pastry blender. Sprinkle 3 to 4 tblsp. cold orange juice over crumb mixture, a little at a time, tossing with a fork until dough forms. Press dough firmly into a ball.

STRAWBERRY PIE

Microwaved Pie Shell (recipe follows)	1 tblsp. lemon juice
⅓ c. sugar	2 pt. fresh strawberries, hulled
4½ tsp. cornstarch	Sweetened whipped cream
1 (10-oz.) pkg. frozen strawberries, thawed	

Prepare Microwaved Pie Shell.

Combine sugar and cornstarch in small glass bowl. Stir in thawed strawberries.

Microwave (high setting) 2 minutes. Stir. Microwave 2 to 3 minutes more, or until mixture thickens, stirring after each minute. Stir in lemon juice. Cool slightly.

Arrange fresh strawberries, stem ends down, in Microwaved Pie Shell. Spoon sauce evenly over strawberries.

Refrigerate at least 2 hours. To serve, top with puffs of sweetened whipped cream. Makes 8 servings.

Microwaved Pie Shell: Combine 1¼ c. unsifted flour and dash of salt in bowl. Cut in ½ c. regular margarine until coarse crumbs form, using a pastry blender. Sprinkle 2 to 3 tblsp. iced water over crumb mixture a little at a time, tossing with a fork until dough forms. Press firmly into a ball.

Roll out dough on floured surface to 13″ circle. Fit loosely into 9″ glass pie plate. Gently press out air pockets, using your fingertips. Trim edge to 1″ beyond rim of pie plate. Fold under edge of crust and form a ridge. Flute edge. Refrigerate 30 minutes.

Prick surface of pie shell with a fork. Microwave (high setting) 3 minutes. Rotate plate one-half turn. Microwave 3 to 4 minutes more, or until pastry is dry and opaque. (Cover any brown spots as they appear with small pieces of aluminum foil.) Cool on rack.

FRESH APRICOT CHIFFON PIE

Gingersnap Crust (recipe
  follows)
1 env. plus 1 tsp.
  unflavored gelatin
¼ c. cold water
½ c. sugar
2 tblsp. cornstarch
2 c. milk
2 eggs, separated

2 tsp. vanilla
½ tsp. almond extract
¼ tsp. cream of tartar
⅓ c. sugar
1 c. heavy cream,
  whipped
3 tblsp. apricot preserves
8 medium apricots,
  pared and quartered

Prepare Gingersnap Crust. Sprinkle gelatin over water.

Combine ½ c. sugar and cornstarch in 1½-qt. glass casserole. Stir in milk. Microwave (high setting) 7 minutes or until thick and bubbly, stirring every 2 minutes.

Beat egg yolks slightly. Stir a small amount of hot mixture into yolks. Stir yolk mixture back into hot mixture. Microwave (medium setting) 1 minute. Stir in softened gelatin, vanilla and almond extract. Chill until it has the consistency of unbeaten egg whites.

Beat egg whites and cream of tartar in bowl until foamy, using an electric mixer at high speed. Gradually add ⅓ c. sugar, beating until stiff, glossy peaks form. Fold in whipped cream. When gelatin mixture mounds when dropped from a spoon, fold into egg white mixture. Turn into crust and refrigerate until set.

Place preserves in glass measuring cup. Microwave (high setting) 45 seconds, or until bubbles appear around edge. Arrange apricots around edge of pie. Spoon warm preserves over apricots. Refrigerate 1 hour before serving. Makes 6 to 8 servings.

Gingersnap Crust: Combine 1½ c. gingersnap crumbs and ⅓ c. butter or regular margarine (melted) in bowl; mix well. Press into 9″ glass pie plate. Refrigerate until ready to fill.

PUMPKIN CHEESE PIE

Graham Cracker Crust
(recipe follows)
4 (3-oz.) pkg. cream
cheese, softened
¾ c. packed brown sugar
2 tblsp. flour
1 tsp. grated lemon rind
1 tsp. pumpkin pie spice

¼ tsp. vanilla
3 eggs
1 c. cooked or canned
mashed pumpkin
¾ c. dairy sour cream
1 tblsp. sugar
¼ tsp. vanilla
Ground nutmeg

Prepare Graham Cracker Crust.

Cream together cream cheese and brown sugar in bowl until light and fluffy, using an electric mixer at medium speed. Blend in flour, lemon rind, pumpkin pie spice and ¼ tsp. vanilla. Add eggs, one at a time, beating well after each addition. Blend in pumpkin. Pour mixture into Graham Cracker Crust.

Microwave (medium setting) 18 minutes, or until center is set, rotating dish one-quarter turn every 3 minutes.

Combine sour cream, sugar and ¼ tsp. vanilla in bowl; mix well. Spread mixture over hot pie and sprinkle with nutmeg. Cool on rack.

Refrigerate 3 hours before serving. Makes 8 servings.

Graham Cracker Crust: Combine 1½ c. graham cracker crumbs, ⅓ c. butter or regular margarine (melted) and ½ tsp. pumpkin pie spice in bowl; mix well. Press into 9" glass pie plate. Refrigerate until ready to fill.

CHERRY TARTS

Microwaved Tart Pastry
(recipe follows)
Sugar
1 (16-oz.) can tart red
cherries in water
6 tblsp. sugar

1½ tblsp. cornstarch
⅛ tsp. salt
⅛ tsp. almond extract
10 drops red food
coloring

Prepare Microwaved Tart Pastry and roll out on floured surface to ⅛" thickness. Cut 6 rounds, using a floured 5" round cookie cutter. Cut 6 decorative shapes from remaining pastry. Fit rounds over inverted 6-oz. glass custard cups. Prick surface of shells with a fork. Arrange cups in a ring in microwave oven. Microwave (high setting) 3 minutes. Rearrange cups. Microwave 2 minutes more, or until pastry is dry and opaque. (Cover any brown spots with small pieces of aluminum foil.) Cool on rack.

Carefully loosen pastry with spatula and remove from cups. Sprinkle pastry cut-outs with sugar and place on waxed paper. Microwave (high setting) 2 to 3 minutes, rotating one-quarter turn after each minute. Cool on rack.

Drain cherries, reserving ½ c. liquid. Combine 6 tblsp. sugar, cornstarch and salt in glass bowl. Stir in cherries, ½ c. reserved liquid, almond extract and food coloring.

Microwave (high setting) 3 minutes. Stir. Microwave 3 minutes more, or until mixture boils and thickens, stirring after each minute. Spoon cherry mixture into tart shells. Cool on rack. Top each tart with a pastry cut-out. Makes 6 tarts.

Microwaved Tart Pastry: Combine 1¼ c. sifted flour and ½ tsp. salt in bowl. Cut in ½ c. regular margarine until coarse crumbs form. Sprinkle 2 to 3 tblsp. iced water over crumb mixture, tossing with a fork until dough forms. Press into a ball.

BLUEBERRY SHORTCAKES

½ c. light corn syrup
¼ c. lemon juice
¼ c. water
4 c. fresh blueberries
1 tsp. grated lemon rind
2 c. sifted flour
¼ c. sugar
3 tsp. baking powder
½ tsp. salt

½ c. shortening
1 egg
⅓ c. milk
2 tblsp. butter or regular
   margarine, melted
⅓ c. graham cracker
   crumbs
Sweetened whipped
   cream

Combine corn syrup, lemon juice and water in 2-qt. glass casserole. Microwave (high setting) 3 minutes, or until mixture comes to a boil. Stir in blueberries and ½ tsp. of the lemon rind. Set aside.

Sift together flour, ¼ c. sugar, baking powder and salt in bowl. Cut in shortening until coarse crumbs form.

Combine egg, milk and remaining ½ tsp. lemon rind in bowl; beat with a fork. Add to dry ingredients all at once, stirring with a fork just until soft dough forms.

Turn dough out onto floured surface and knead lightly 8 to 10 times. Roll out dough to ½" thickness. Cut with floured 3" round cookie cutter. Dip rounds in butter. Then roll in graham cracker crumbs. Place 4 rounds in a ring in 10" glass pie plate.

Microwave (high setting) 2½ to 3 minutes or until dry and puffy, rotating plate one-half turn after each minute. Repeat with remaining rounds.

Split hot shortcakes and place bottom halves on dessert plates. Spoon some of the blueberry mixture over each. Top each with remaining shortcake halves, remaining blueberry mixture and sweetened whipped cream. Makes 8 servings.

BUTTERSCOTCH BANANA SPLITS

1½ c. packed brown sugar	3 medium bananas,
⅓ c. light cream	diagonally sliced
⅓ c. light corn syrup	1 qt. vanilla ice cream
¼ c. butter or regular	Sweetened whipped
margarine	cream
1 tsp. vanilla	Toasted slivered almonds

Combine brown sugar, light cream, corn syrup, butter and vanilla in 2-qt. glass casserole. Microwave (high setting) 1 minute. Stir. Microwave 1½ minutes more, or until bubbles begin to appear around edge. Let stand 5 minutes.

Stir in bananas. Serve warm over vanilla ice cream. Top each serving with sweetened whipped cream and toasted slivered almonds. Makes 6 servings.

CHOCOLATE FONDUE

**8 (1-oz.) squares unsweet-
ened chocolate, cut up
2½ c. sugar
1½ c. light cream
⅔ c. butter or regular
margarine
¼ c. Cointreau or other
orange liqueur**

**Dippers: strawberries,
slices of apples, pears
and peaches; chunks of
pineapple and banana;
ladyfingers; angel food
cake cubes, marsh-
mallows**

Place chocolate in 2-qt. glass casserole. Microwave (medium setting) 2 minutes. Stir. Microwave 2 minutes more or until melted.

Stir in sugar, light cream and butter. Microwave (medium setting) 8 minutes, or until mixture thickens and sugar is dissolved, stirring every 2 minutes. Stir in Cointreau. Pour into fondue pot or chafing dish to keep warm.

Pass a selection of dippers to dip into fondue. If fondue becomes too thick, stir in a little warm light cream. Makes 4 c. or 12 servings.

SUMMER FRUIT FLAMBÉ

⅓ c. sugar
1 tblsp. cornstarch
¾ c. orange juice
¾ c. water
1 (1″) cinnamon stick
½ tsp. grated orange rind
2 tblsp. butter or regular
   margarine

2 large peaches, peeled
   and sliced (about ¾ lb.)
½ lb. Bing cherries,
   halved and pitted
2 medium bananas,
   diagonally sliced
¼ c. Cointreau or other
   orange liqueur

Combine sugar and cornstarch in 2-qt. glass casserole. Stir in orange juice, water, cinnamon stick and orange rind.

Microwave (high setting) 2 minutes. Stir. Microwave 2½ minutes more, or until mixture thickens. Gently stir in butter.

Stir in peaches and microwave (high setting) 1 minute. Stir. Microwave 1 minute more, or until peaches are almost tender. Add cherries and bananas and microwave 1 minute. Remove cinnamon stick.

Place Cointreau in glass measuring cup and microwave (high setting) 15 seconds or until warm. Pour over fruit and ignite with a match. Quickly spoon into dessert dishes. Makes 6 servings.

INDEX